COMPANIONS in Christ®

Mary Ellen Jensen

So much more!

Companions in Christ® is so much more than printed resou~
of people on a journey together. Our Companions We~
journey through

- Opportunities to find other churches offering Con. ~rist groups for youth, children, and adults;
- Insights and testimonies from other Companions in Christ participants;
- Training opportunities that develop and deepen the leadership skills used in formational groups;
- Helpful leadership tips, articles, and downloadable resources;
- A regular e-newsletter offering spiritual formation insights and discounts on Companions resources;
- A promise to pray for your Companions group. For more information, see the "Prayers for Our *Way of Discernment* Group" page in the Leader's Guide.

Just complete this form and drop it in the mail to register yourself and your Companions group on the Companions Web site. Or visit the Web site (www.CompanionsinChrist.org) and enter your information there.

Name _____

Address _____

City/State/Zip _____

Church _____

E-mail _____

Phone _____

____ Please register me to receive the Companions in Christ e-newsletter.
____ Please keep me informed of spiritual formation events and resources from Upper Room Ministries.

COMPANIONS in Christ.

Upper Room Ministries
P.O. Box 340012
Nashville, TN 37203-9540

With deep gratitude and affection
Upper Room Ministries dedicates
this book to the memory of Schuyler Bissell—
man of profound faith and integrity;
advisory group member, trainer, leader;
member of St. George's Episcopal Church, Nashville, Tennessee;
and unflagging advocate
for Companions in Christ.

COMPANIONS *in Christ*
A SMALL-GROUP EXPERIENCE IN SPIRITUAL FORMATION

The Way of DISCERNMENT

Participant's Book

Stephen V. Doughty with Marjorie J. Thompson

UPPER ROOM BOOKS®
NASHVILLE

THE WAY OF DISCERNMENT Participant's Book
A *Companions in Christ* resource
Copyright © 2008 by Upper Room Books®
All rights reserved.

The Upper Room® Web site: www.upperroom.org

At the time of publication, all Web sites referenced in this book were valid. However, due to the fluid nature of the Internet, some addresses may have changed, or the content may no longer be relevant.

Cover design: Left Coast Design, Portland, Oregon
Cover photograph: jupiterimages.com
First printing: 2008

ISBN 978-0-8358-9958-1

Printed in the United States of America

For more information on *Companions in Christ*,
visit www.CompanionsinChrist.org or call 1-800-972-0433.

Contents

Acknowledgments

The original twenty-eight-week *Companions in Christ* resource grew from the seeds of a vision long held by Stephen D. Bryant, publisher of Upper Room Ministries, and given shape by Marjorie J. Thompson, director of Upper Room's Pathways in Congregational Spirituality and spiritual director to Companions in Christ. The vision, which has now expanded into the Companions in Christ series, was realized through the efforts of many people over many years. The original advisers, consultants, authors, editors, and test churches are acknowledged in the foundational resource. We continue to be grateful to each person and congregation named.

Stephen V. Doughty wrote the articles in this Participant's Book. The daily exercises are principally the work of Marjorie Thompson. Marjorie also wrote *The Way of Discernment Leader's Guide*, developing portions based on preliminary suggestions from Stephen Doughty. Consultants included Stephen Bryant, Lynne Deming, Jerry Haas, and Susan Ruach. The Board of Worshipful Work provided valuable input for the development of this project: Kathryn Damiano, Eileen Goor, Tara Hornbacker, Charles Tollett, Connie Wilson, and Don Zimmer. Thanks also to seven test group leaders in four churches whose feedback helped reshape elements of both the Participant's Book and Leader's Guide: Carmen Gaud and Diana Hynson, Edgehill United Methodist Church, Nashville, Tennessee; Amy Hutchinson-Cox and Linda Morley, Second Presbyterian Church, Nashville; Mary Jayne Allen, First Baptist Church of Chattanooga, Tennessee; and Rosita Echols and Jo Ann Powell, Westminster Presbyterian Church, Knoxville, Tennessee.

Introduction

Welcome to *Companions in Christ: The Way of Discernment*, a small-group resource designed to help you explore the nature and practice of spiritual discernment. Interest in discernment has been growing significantly in the church for more than a decade now. Individuals seek personal discernment for vocational decisions and life-changing turns of direction. Church leaders seek the Spirit's guidance for clarity on their congregations' distinctive purpose and mission in the world. Whole denominations search for God's will in matters of doctrine, ethics, and faithful living. An ancient spiritual practice in both Jewish and Christian traditions, discernment is once again being recognized and embraced as a timely and practical means of grace.

In response to the desire of many small groups to continue exploring spiritual practices that began with the original twenty-eight-week *Companions in Christ* resource, Upper Room Ministries has developed the Companions in Christ series. *The Way of Discernment* is the eighth title in the series. It offers a ten-week journey (plus a preparatory meeting) of exploring perspectives and practices for personal spiritual discernment, along with several forms of small-group discernment. Finally, it points beyond the limitations of this small-group process to possibilities for discerning God's will in congregations and larger bodies of the church. We commend it to leadership groups interested in bringing this important practice into congregational and denominational life.

In addition to the foundational twenty-eight-week resource, previous titles in the Companions series include *Exploring the Way*, a six-week introduction to the Christian spiritual journey; *The Way of Grace*, a nine-week walk through central stories in the Gospel of John about encounters with Jesus; *The Way of Blessedness*, a nine-week pilgrimage through the Beatitudes; *The Way of Forgiveness*, an eight-week exploration of the forgiven and forgiving life; *The Way of Transforming Discipleship*, a six-week journey plus a closing pilgrimage retreat through which participants experience more deeply what it means to live as a Christ-follower; and *The Way of Prayer*, a ten-week experience in expanding group members' vision and practice of prayer.

With the exception of *Exploring the Way*, each resource in the Companions series expands on the content of the original twenty-eight-week resource and uses the same basic format. *Companions in Christ* explored the Christian spiritual life under five headings: Journey, Scripture, Prayer, Call, and Spiritual Guidance. Each supplementary volume in the series explores in greater depth some aspect of one of these areas of spiritual life and practice. *The Way of Discernment* falls under the general heading of Spiritual Guidance, although it also has close affinity with the category of Call.

As discerning people of faith, our journeys remain rooted in a biblical understanding of God's wisdom and guidance. When we ponder scripture in a Companions group, we engage the stories and texts with our whole selves—intellect, emotion, intuition, and will—as we draw on classic practices of scriptural meditation, prayer, and journaling. It is important to understand that Companions does not offer Bible study in any traditional sense. It represents a more experiential, formational approach to scripture than an informational approach. We are interested in exploring discernment as a pathway of spiritual formation, discovering how seeking divine wisdom helps shape us into the fullness of the image of Christ.

Like the foundational *Companions in Christ* resource, *The Way of Discernment* will help you deepen essential practices of the Christian life. It focuses on your daily experience of God and your growing capacity to respond to grace with gratitude, trust, love, and self-offering. Because this exploration takes place in the midst of a small group, you can expect increasingly to realize the blessings of mutual support, encouragement, guidance, and accountability in Christian community. Your growth in faith and maturation in discerning will benefit your congregation as well.

About the Resource and Process

Like all Companions resources, *The Way of Discernment* has two primary components: individual reading and daily exercises through the week with this Participant's Book, and a weekly two-hour meeting based on directions in the Leader's Guide.

Each weekly chapter in the Participant's Book introduces new material and five daily exercises to help you reflect on your life in light of the chapter content. After your group's Preparatory Meeting, you will begin a weekly cycle as follows: On Day 1 you will read the article; on Days 2–6 you will complete the five daily exercises found at the end of the chapter; on Day 7 you will meet with your group.

The daily exercises aim to help you move from information (knowledge *about*) to experience (knowledge *of*). The time commitment for one daily exercise is approximately twenty to thirty minutes. An important part of this process is keeping a personal notebook or journal in which you record reflections, prayers, and questions for later review and for reference at the weekly group meeting.

Weekly meetings begin and end with simple worship times, and they include time for sharing reflections on the exercises of the past week and for moving deeper into the content of the article through various learning and prayer experiences. Although the time commitment for meetings is generally two hours, note that the final meeting for *The Way of Discernment* will run about twenty minutes longer in order to bring adequate closure to your group process. You will need to bring your Participant's Book, your Bible, and your personal notebook or journal to each weekly group meeting.

A unique feature of *The Way of Discernment* is the inclusion of a simple but penetrating question to reflect on throughout the coming week, in addition to the reading and daily exercises. Requiring just a few minutes each day, this reflection question will give you a taste of living with one deep question over time. During the Sharing Insights period of the next meeting, your group will have opportunity to share significant insights around this question of the week, building an experiential foundation for the practice of group discernment.

The Companions in Christ Web Site

Another dimension of resources in the Companions series is the Web site. The Companions in Christ Web site is designed to provide information on the entire Companions family of resources (children, youth, and adults). The site offers helpful information for leaders, group members, and those desiring more information about involvement in Companions. Visit www.CompanionsinChrist.org.

Your Personal Notebook or Journal

Keeping a journal or personal notebook (commonly called journaling) will be one of the most important dimensions of your personal experience with *The Way of Discernment.* The Participant's Book gives you daily spiritual exercises each week. Often you will be asked to note your thoughts, feelings, questions, or prayers in relation to the exercise. Upper Room Books offers a *Companions in Christ Journal* that you may wish to purchase. (To order the journal, go to www.upperroom.org/bookstore or call 1-800-972-0433.) You will want, at a minimum, something more permanent than a ring binder or notepad.

Even if you are inexperienced with journaling, you may quickly find it becoming second nature. Your thoughts may start to pour out, giving expression to an inner life that has never been released. But should you find the writing difficult or cumbersome, give yourself permission to try it in a new way. Since a journal is for your eyes only, you may choose any style that suits you. You need not worry about using beautiful words, good grammar, spelling, or even complete sentences! Jotting down key ideas, insights, or musings in a few words or phrases is just fine. You might doodle while you think, or sketch an image that comes to you. Make journaling fun and relaxed! Remember, you have complete freedom to share with the group only what you choose of your reflections.

Keeping a journal as you move through *The Way of Discernment* is important for two reasons. First, the process of writing down thoughts clarifies them for us. They become more specific and concrete. Sometimes we really don't know what we think until we see our thoughts on paper, and often the process of writing generates new insight. Second, this personal record captures our inward experience over time so we can track changes in our thinking and growth. Memories are notoriously fragile and fleeting; specific feelings or creative connections we had two weeks ago or even three days ago can be hard to recall without a written record. Though your journal cannot capture all that goes through your mind in a single reflection period, it will offer reminders you can draw on during small-group meetings each week.

When you begin a daily exercise, have your journal and pen at hand. Learn to stop and write as you go, thinking on paper. Feel free to write anything that comes to you. If the process seems clumsy at first, keep an open mind. Like any spiritual practice, journaling gets easier over time, and its value becomes more apparent.

Your weekly practice of journaling is shaped as follows: On the day after your group meeting, read the next week's article. Jot down your "aha!" moments, questions, disagreements, images, or other reflections. You may prefer to note these in the margins of the Participant's Book. Over the next five days, do the exercises for the week, recording responses in your journal. On the day of the group meeting, review what you have written through the week, marking portions you would like to share in the group. Bring your journal to meetings so you can refer to it directly or refresh your memory about thoughts you want to paraphrase. You may find your journal helps you discern more clearly your own calling and how God is at work in your life.

Your Group Meeting

The weekly meeting is divided into four segments. First you will gather for a brief time of worship called the Opening, which allows you to set aside the concerns of the day and focus on God's guiding presence as you begin the group session.

The second segment of the meeting is called Sharing Insights. During this time the group leader will invite you to talk about your experiences with the reading and daily exercises. The leader will participate as a member and share his or her responses as well. Generally each member will briefly share thoughts and insights related to specific exercises. This process helps the group learn and practice what it means to listen deeply. You are a community of persons seeking to listen to God and to one another so that you can live more faithfully as disciples of Jesus Christ. The group provides a supportive community to explore your listening, your spiritual practices, and your efforts to employ those practices in daily life, including your life in the church.

This community does not function as a traditional support group, where people are sometimes quick to offer advice or comment on one another's experiences. In a Companions group, members try to honor one another's experiences through prayerful attentiveness; affirmation; and respectful, clarifying questions. The Sharing Insights part of the meeting is less meaningful when persons interrupt and comment on what is being said, trying to correct or fix what they see as a problem (such comments are called "cross talk," meaning that we talk across one another). Group members are instead invited to trust the Holy Spirit's guidance and help one another listen to that guidance within one's own spirit and in and through one another's words.

The Sharing Insights time presents a unique opportunity to learn how God works differently in each person's life. Our spiritual journeys, while varied, enrich others' experiences. Other people's faith stories allow us to see anew how God's activity touches or addresses our lives in unexpected ways. The group will establish some ground rules to facilitate this sharing. Participants need to agree clearly that each person will speak only about his or her own beliefs, feelings, and responses and that all group members have permission to share only what they choose and when they feel ready to share. Above all, the group should maintain confidentiality so that what is shared stays in the group. Spouses or close friends in the same group will need to agree between themselves on permissible boundaries of confidentiality so that the choice to reveal one's self does not inadvertently reveal intimacies to the group without the other's consent.

The leader participates in this sharing, while also listening and summarizing key insights that have surfaced. The leader closes this part of the meeting by inviting attention to any patterns or themes that seem to have emerged from the group sharing. These patterns may point to a word God is offering to the group.

The third segment of the meeting is called Deeper Explorations. This part of the meeting gives group members an opportunity to explore a deeper dimension of God's grace, to practice related spiritual disciplines, or to explore implications of the week's theme for their church. In *The Way of Discernment*, the focus gradually shifts from personal practice to group practice and finally to broader church practices.

As it began, the group meeting ends with a brief time of worship called the Closing. Here members may offer prayers of thanks or concern that arise from the meeting or express the spiritual learning of the week through symbol and ritual.

Invitation to the Journey

We cannot journey far into the terrain of discernment unaccompanied by the risen Lord, our true and present guide in every dimension of Christian discipleship. The goal of the Christian life is to become fully the persons God created us to be, which means becoming—each in our own way—more and more like Jesus Christ, "the image of the invisible God" (Col. 1:15). It is the great work and delight of the Holy Spirit to conform us to Christ (2 Cor. 3:18). The weeks we give to *The Way of Discernment* offer a unique opportunity to focus on our relationship with the Holy Spirit, through whom we receive God's guiding presence both personally and together.

So now we invite you to seek the grace of the Spirit as you begin *The Way of Discernment*. Open your heart inwardly to all God desires to pour out upon you and your companions on the journey as you explore together the gift of discernment. Enter this experience with joyful anticipation of God's rich blessings! May the Holy Spirit guide your footsteps as you follow in the way of Christ.

Week 1

The Beckoning of Discernment

Make me to know your ways, O LORD;
teach me your paths.

—Psalm 25:4

What I most recall about my friend that afternoon is the expression on his face. For days he had struggled with a difficult decision. Never one to knit his brow or look long-faced, he kept his most serious wrestling out of sight. This present search had been no exception. Still, in recent days he had grown unusually quiet, bordering on withdrawn. As he approached me now, his eyes looked outward, warm, utterly relaxed. To my, "How are you doing today?" he answered, "I've discerned." He smiled quietly and continued. "This won't be the end of it, but I know what I need to do. It's all a gift."

My friend always chose words carefully. "I've discerned" was an unusual response. He might have said, "I've decided what to do," but instead went for "discerned." He could have charged into telling me his plans, but simply ended saying what a gift he had been given. I knew him well enough to glean that "discerned" and "gift" pointed to a lot of prayer, a lot of reaching after God's will in the situation that faced him, and, quite likely, a lot of waiting.

He was right when he said, "This won't be the end of it." Over the years it has become plain that his discernment was just a beginning. And coming back to what I most remember, it is clear that the expression on his face that afternoon mirrored what continues to be true: although some say his discernment cost him dearly, he is at peace and knows he has followed in the way God beckoned him.

I have at times envied my friend. Indeed, who of us has not at some point wished to see clearly the path we need to take? Who of us has not longed to discern God's will in the midst of clouded or difficult circumstances? It is precisely here that what we call discernment starts to beckon us. It beckons as a deeply felt desire. It beckons as a path toward greater understanding and comes as a gift. When we pay attention to the attractions of this desire, this path, this gift, we begin to see—as my friend clearly saw—why we want to grow in the way of discernment.

A Desire

Before we ever hear the word *discernment*, its reality beckons us. Long ahead of our efforts to understand its meaning, the need for discernment tugs at us. It meets us in our most profound yearning. It calls to us through our deep desire to walk in ways that are whole, right, fitting for our lives.

Some of us use religious language to name this desire for discernment. "I want to do the will of God here," we say. Or, drawing on a slightly different tradition, we say, "I want to follow God's plan for my life." Desire may well up in a prayer that cries out from the heart, "Loving God, *please* show me which way I should follow!" The word *discern* may not pass our lips, but the desire to move faithfully in God's way burns within us. We speak that desire in the language of a faith we have perhaps sought to follow for years or are perhaps just beginning to pursue.

Some of us use no words at all to express the desire. The term *God* may not, for the moment, cross our mind. We simply feel a deep longing. With all that is in us, we strain for a clearer vision of what will lead us toward wholeness, true fulfillment, or a sense of rightness in life.

Discernment often beckons when we face life's vital choices. We fall in love and wonder, *Is this the person I should marry and seek to grow with through all the years that lie ahead?* Or we suffer wrenching abuse in a relationship and struggle with the questions: "What is the most faithful thing to do now? For the sake of those around me, for my own sake, what should I do?" At key points in our lives, we consider our gifts, passions, joys, and we ask, "What can I do that will most honor what God has given me?" We face a specific career choice or receive an invitation to

Seek instruction . . . so as to know what the Lord's will is. Life and death [are] laid before you. Whichever you will choose will be given to you.

—Soetken van den Houte

take on a role that may look overwhelming, and we must decide, "Will I accept this job or should I turn it aside?" In all these circumstances, discernment beckons us, even if we do not know or use the term.

Discernment pulls at us in the midst of life's changes. A loved one dies, and we ask searching questions. "How can I constructively fill my days now? How might I faithfully give what I have to offer in this new season of life?" A child is born, and we wonder, *How shall I live in a way that brings goodness and guidance to this little one who looks to me?* We suddenly fall ill or unexpectedly get well, and we wonder, *How shall I live during the time given to me?*

On the deepest level, the need to discern asserts itself whenever we yearn to find the most fulfilling aim and pattern for our lives. "What manner of living will bring me closest to my real purpose for being?" "How can I most fruitfully spend the gift of my days?" In our rushed society we too seldom ask such questions. The hubbub and pressure of activities distract us. Yet whenever these questions break through, they halt us in our tracks, and we find ourselves beckoned into the way of discernment.

On the simplest level, the need to discern arises amidst ordinary daily circumstances and choices. "What are the most important priorities for me this week?" "How can I discover a more constructive response to this child's behavior next time around?" We sometimes don't think of such practical decisions as matters requiring discernment, yet the impulse to seek a deeper wisdom and awareness in day-to-day matters reveals, again, the allure of discernment.

On the broadest level, the need to discern takes hold as a yearning, not just in our personal lives, but also in the life we share in community. Our family may need to decide a new direction together. The church we belong to may strain for a fresh vision of its mission. The denomination we are a part of may struggle to rediscover its unity in Christ. We may join a small group that seeks fresh ways to receive and share the life-changing gifts of the poor and the outcast among us. In communities such as these, the need for discernment tugs at us yet again.

At its root and foundation, both personally and with others, discernment calls to us through simple, raw desire—desire to find the right way, to choose the right path, to gain clarity about our God-given purpose and what we can offer to the world around us.

The need for discernment arises out of the natural flow of life and its challenges.
—Jeannette Bakke

To discern is to sift through the illusory. It is to come to discover what is real.
—Rose Mary Dougherty

A Path

Even as discernment beckons through our inmost desires, it stretches out as a path before us and invites us to enter. The word *discernment* itself implies the existence of a pathway toward greater clarity in our times of wondering. It comes from the Latin *discernere,* meaning "to separate," "to distinguish." The word *discernment* denotes an activity or process. It suggests that when we yearn to find what is right and fitting, there will be a means to do so. On the most elemental level, to discern is to sort and sift through the possibilities when we face a variety of choices. It is to distinguish and separate the alternatives. The very word *discernment* thus suggests a helpful means of going forward.

From deep within ourselves we sense a desire to engage in right actions, to make wise choices, to live in a fruitful manner. Then from beyond ourselves we begin to hear, "Look, there is a way you can follow that leads toward greater understanding. There are steps you can take that will open you to the clarity you seek." We stand before the forest of our own wonderings. Then bit by bit, we become aware of a path through the forest.

Many of us have caught hints of this path in simple practices we learned during our earliest years or picked up from persons wiser than ourselves. We make a decision but then say, "I'm going to sleep on it." Somewhere we gleaned the wisdom that a good night's rest brings fresh vision. We struggle with a difficult choice and say, "I really need the perspective of a trusted friend," or "I am going to take time to consider where my decision might lead in the long run." When we engage in such practices, we do so with the sense that there is at least a partial path through our wondering.

The scriptures repeatedly acknowledge the existence of a sure pathway in life and greatly expand our understanding of what it is about. On becoming king of Israel, young Solomon earnestly prays to the Lord: "Give your servant therefore an understanding mind to govern your people, able to discern between good and evil; for who can govern this your great people?" (1 Kings 3:9). Solomon recognizes that knowing good from evil lies at the heart of discernment. Jesus carries the matter even farther. When Peter sees great good in Jesus continuing his ministry, Jesus rebukes him for failing to see the still greater good God desires to give (Matt. 16:21-23). In the full vision of the scriptures, discernment

You have made us for yourself, and our heart is restless until it rests in you.

—Saint Augustine

requires not just that we distinguish between good and evil, but even between one good and another. Faithful discernment thrusts upon us that piercing question, What is the higher good?

"Do not be conformed to this world," writes the apostle Paul to the Christians at Rome, "but be transformed by the renewing of your minds, so that you may discern what is the will of God—what is good and acceptable and perfect" (Rom. 12:2). Discernment is about more than taking this or that course of action in life, more than deciding whether to give time to this cause or that project. Discernment is ultimately about doing the will of the living God. Paul enjoins his listeners to follow a way of sorting, sifting, seeing clearly the desires of God. In a similar vein, the author of the First Letter of John writes, "Beloved, do not believe every spirit, but test the spirits to see whether they are from God" (1 John 4:1).

Such scriptural references are demanding, yet they also serve as encouragement. They remind us that in even the most exacting circumstances lies a way, a path that leads to greater understanding of God's desire and therefore of what we are to do.

A Gift

Discernment calls to us in our own deep yearnings. It beckons as a pathway we can take in response to these yearnings. Finally, discernment comes to us as a gift, pure and simple.

Shortly before writing these pages, I heard a friend talk about the place of discernment in her community of faith. Her community is less than a decade old. From the start, its members decided to practice discernment. "We had no idea what we were doing or what we were getting ourselves into!" she said. Nonetheless, community members sought to learn the art of discernment and to grow in its practice both personally and in their life together.

"Now we laugh a lot when we discern," my friend said. "It is a pure gift when insights come and clarity grows. We can't *make* this happen, yet it does. And the practice of discernment itself is such a gift. Independent of any specific issues we wrestle with and any particular insights we receive, discernment allows God to shape us into something new."

My friend's words accented the twofold nature of discernment as gift. First, the coming of insight itself is a gift. Many of us know this from our own experience. We pray for deeper understanding. We wait. We struggle. We search. Then, aha! Understanding comes. Perhaps it flares forth suddenly. Perhaps it emerges with the slow, growing radiance of the morning sun. Either way, we know we have not brought the insight into being ourselves. It comes from beyond us. It arrives as a treasure, and we rejoice at its appearance.

Second, the very process of arriving at the insight is a gift. Through prayerfulness, waiting, struggle, and resting in the unknown, we have been formed. We are not the same as before. All this too is a gift. So there is gift in the practice and gift in the result. Discernment is both effort and grace, method and fruit, verb and noun. When my friend said, "Discernment is such a gift," these shimmering elements danced together in her smile.

In the sixteenth century, Ignatius of Loyola, founder of the Jesuits, designed a rich set of guidelines for what he called "the discernment of spirits." The Ignatian guidelines invite specific activities of reasoning and prayerful reflection, and comprise one of the most developed and practical pathways of discernment available to us. The Jesuits are acknowledged masters of method, yet they are absolutely clear that discernment is finally a gift. Contemporary Jesuit priest and teacher Thomas H. Green has observed that discernment "is a gift, not primarily the fruit of personal effort, but God's gift to those who love and are loved by [God]."[1]

Seeing discernment as a gift puts all our efforts in perspective. Yes, we follow certain counsels of wisdom as we seek to discern. We engage in specific processes, take particular steps. From one angle of vision, we rightly see discernment as a pathway or method. Yet that method cannot guarantee that, with sufficient personal effort, we will arrive at clarity. It is not even a pathway we take accompanied by God so that we may, with a bit of help, attain a sharper vision. We take the pathway simply and solely to prepare ourselves to receive the gift of discernment however and wherever it comes.

Seeing discernment as a gift also helps us know the priceless value of what God offers us in it. What beckons is not just greater clarity on some

We often equate discernment with a skill which we must master rather than the gift of God's love which guides us home to Love.

—Rose Mary Dougherty

issue with which we struggle. A desire for clarity may mark the beginning of our journey into discernment, and an enriched understanding may be part of the gift we receive. But what calls to us from discernment is far deeper than just one piece of knowing. What summons us is a whole way of being shaped afresh by God through all our living and searching. This, as we shall soon explore, is a process of being formed by the grace of the Spirit in accord with God's yearning for us and for all of creation. Being so shaped is a gift indeed!

Looking Ahead

Another Way had to be found and explored.
—Malcolm Muggeridge

The following chapters focus on preparing ourselves to receive a gift. At no point will they present a tidy recipe for discernment. You will not read, "Do A, B, and C, and then you will know precisely God's will for you." Rather, you will meet a variety of teachings, perspectives, and counsels that can open us all to being formed by God. This formation takes place in our most turbulent wondering, and it happens equally well where life seems pleasantly or wretchedly settled. Discernment gifts us with a way of being shaped through all the seasons of our lives—the calm, the wild, and those when we must live for a long time with our most perplexing questions.

Recent years have seen rising interest in communal discernment. In Weeks 7 and 8 we will pay particular attention to discerning with others. Yet in a very real sense, we never discern alone. We need to share our questions and insights with others along the way. We draw from the learning of those who have gone before us. Even our most private struggles enrich the community, and the public searching of the community enriches us personally. So let us begin the exploration, knowing we are not alone.

DAILY EXERCISES

Before beginning these exercises, read Week 1, "The Beckoning of Discernment." Make notes in your journal as you read, recording thoughts, prayers, and questions. Do the same as you engage in these reflection exercises.

Limiting yourself to one exercise a day will make this practice more meaningful. Give yourself the gift of a sanctuary of quiet time and space to engage these spiritual reflections in a prayerful, unrushed way. Expect to spend at least twenty minutes on each exercise, with an upper limit of thirty minutes so it does not become burdensome. Open yourself to the very real presence and leading of God's Spirit.

EXERCISE 1

Read Psalm 25:4-10. This prayer expresses the psalmist's profound yearning to know God's way, to follow the Lord's path through the treacherous twists and turns of life.

Ponder these verses. In your journal, list key words or phrases that speak to your heart. What does this psalm say to you about the nature of discernment?

Now reflect on your own yearning to know God's path through your life. What guidance from God do you seek in your life just now? How would you name it?

Write a prayer or psalm expressing your longing to know God's path in your life.

EXERCISE 2

Read 1 Kings 3:5-12. This text describes Solomon's request for wisdom to govern God's people, as well as the Lord's delighted response to the young king.

Reflect on some reasons people seek discernment, including your own reasons. Note them in your journal. Which seem more personal, and which are more directed to the common or public good?

Where do you desire wisdom in order to give yourself more fully in service to others? Spend some time praying about this. Note thoughts or questions in your journal.

EXERCISE 3

Read Proverbs 1:1-4. The book of Proverbs, attributed to Solomon, begins by listing some of the king's reasons for seeking God's wisdom. Compare them with the reasons for discernment you listed in Exercise 2 and see what you notice.

Now read Proverbs 14:21-35. This book collects many ancient Hebrew wisdom sayings, of which these verses are representative. Write down some of the wise sayings you gleaned from parents, teachers, or friends as you grew up. Which have helped you? Which have steered you off course? Do any suggest a method or path of discernment (e.g., "Sleep on it" or "Don't judge a book by its cover")?

What do you already know and practice as basic principles to follow in making life decisions well? Give thanks to God for these guidelines of wisdom.

EXERCISE 4

Read Matthew 16:13-17. Jesus makes it clear that Peter's declaration of Jesus' true identity was an "aha!" moment, a knowing that came as gift, revealed by "my Father in heaven."

When have you experienced deeper knowledge coming to you as gift—an intuition that turned out to be right, a sudden sense of clarity, a constructive idea you wouldn't normally have thought on your own? Note what you can recall in your journal.

What were the circumstances of each situation, and your state of mind and heart? In retrospect, what do you think you might learn about discernment from such experiences? Jot down your thoughts. Then open yourself in quiet prayer for several minutes to the mystery of God's grace and guidance.

EXERCISE 5

Read Proverbs 11:14 and 12:10-11. Verses like these suggest that discernment is needed at every level of human life, including matters of state and our relationship with the earth and its creatures.

Quiet yourself in God's presence, and let the Spirit speak to your heart about where discernment is particularly needed in our time. List these thoughts in your journal. Then ponder the underlying need behind all these issues. What do you think is the root need or requirement for human discernment of God's way?

Draw an image or symbol in your journal of this root need. Spend some time praying about what you see.

The Heart of Discernment

He has told you, O mortal, what is good;
and what does the LORD require of you
but to do justice, and to love kindness,
and to walk humbly with your God?
—Micah 6:8

At the conclusion of our first week's chapter, we noted that discernment comes as a gift from the living God. As we open ourselves to this gift, it will be helpful to lay certain foundations of understanding by probing more deeply into its nature. Specifically, we will consider three questions that lie at the heart of theological reflection on discernment: How do we understand God as the source of this gift? What do we mean when we speak of "God's will"? What is the ultimate aim or intent of discernment? As we deal with these pivotal questions, we start to see more clearly what discernment is all about. We also prepare ourselves to enter the way of discernment with greater freedom and receptivity.

God as the Source of the Gift

Tom and I were having our regular cup of coffee. We meet early every other Friday morning and have just one cup each. We drink slowly and talk a lot, though the occasional silences are as comfortable for us as speaking. In the past few years, I have come to cherish these times together. A little younger than I, Tom is the superb administrator of a secular agency. A few years ago he received a statewide award for his work on behalf of people living on the margins of society. He might best be described as a "Christian seeker." In matters of faith, as in his work, Tom never pretends to have all the answers. He asks a multitude of searching questions.

Over the years, Tom has also made a number of notably wise decisions, and that was where I wanted to focus our conversation this particular morning. When confronted with difficult choices, how did he decide what to do? How did he maintain his balance amid fiercely competing claims? How did he finally settle on a course of action and manage to do so with the composure and continual openness so evident to those around him? I laid out these questions all at once and pressed him. Tom answered shyly and simply, "I pray." After a bit of quiet, he added with considerable emphasis, "When it comes to dealing with this stuff, I don't do it by myself." He smiled.

The real One who does the discerning is the Holy Spirit.
—Gerald May

"I don't do it by myself." Behind the words and the smile lay a reality on which my friend depended. In the process of weighing, sifting, and sorting possibilities, Tom clearly sensed he was not alone. My honest friend had an aversion to spouting easy pieties, and he did not, at this moment, name God directly. Nonetheless, when it came to discernment, experience told him that its source was Another.

The scriptures and traditional teachings on discernment sharpen our vision of the reality my friend pointed to—that God is the source of the gift. This vision both informs and stretches us. Paul writes in his letter to the Philippians, "It is God who is at work in you, enabling you both to will and to work for his good pleasure" (2:13). While we strain to see the way we should go, God works within us, leading and guiding. This is true even, and perhaps especially, in our places of deep confusion. "Likewise the Spirit helps us in our weakness; for we do not know how to pray as we ought, but that very Spirit intercedes with sighs too deep for words" (Rom. 8:26).

Jesus promises the Holy Spirit to his followers and, in the Greek text of the Gospel of John, describes the Holy Spirit with the word *parakletos*, which means both "advocate" and "helper" (John 14:16). Jesus tells us this Spirit, "whom the Father will send in my name, will teach you everything, and remind you of all that I have said to you" (John 14:26).

The Holy Spirit will point, encourage, and guide us in the way of Jesus and all that he has given us.

As the Spirit reminds us of Jesus, it is the risen and ascended Christ who becomes the source of our discernment. Contemporary Quaker scholar Paul Anderson notes that while Christians widely affirm "the resurrection of Christ, too few have taken seriously what it means to live under his present leadership. In fact, the implications of believing in the resurrected Lord may be among the most neglected aspects of the Christian faith!"[1] Yet Christ's present, "real time" leadership comes as a rich, living guide in our times of discernment if we seek it.[2]

Tom was absolutely right. Our limited minds are not the source of deeper wisdom. We cannot discern what is best by ourselves. Right choices in ambiguous circumstances do not derive from our own hard efforts at reasoning, as important as sound reasoning and conscientious effort may be in opening us to the gift of discernment. The gift itself flows from a Source that far transcends our limited capacities. We may at points meet this Source as a subtle whispering of the Spirit within us. We may come to know it as the Holy Spirit working openly and boldly in our lives. We may encounter it in the risen Christ, present to teach and lead us along the way. None of this, of course, should ease us into simplistic thinking. What it can do, however, is turn us to the One whose will for our lives we seek to know.

What We Mean by God's Will

Over the years I have been impressed by how differently people respond to the phrase "the will of God." Some see it as wonderfully freeing, while others regard it as rigid, heavy, or even fear-inspiring. And I have been equally struck by how I can flip back and forth between these two modes of perceiving God's will. At my most anxious, I conceive of God's will as tightly and precisely fixed. I must sniff it out in every detail. Even when I think I have done so, a cloud darkens my mind. *Am I really doing the right thing here?* At my most free, though, I move forward with confidence about God's intention for my life. I still care deeply about the steps I take, both large and small, but I take them with the sense that as long as I am

[Many] fear that God's will may be the worst thing that could happen. . . . God's will is the best thing that can happen to us under any circumstances.
—Danny Morris and Charles Olsen

moving in the direction of God's love, I am living faithfully and joyfully as I truly wish to.

"I stopped using the phrase 'God's will' some years ago," a parishioner once told me. "I prefer to think of God's *loving longing.*" Because of experiences early in her life, the very phrase "God's will" suggested something harsh and dictatorial. "God's loving longing," she explained, came much closer to expressing the compassionate God she had come to know in her deepening spiritual life.

While some may find this woman's language too soft, phrases like "God's intention" or "God's deep yearning" or even "God's dream" may help open us to the heart of what we mean when we speak of the will of God. To consider God's longing is to pay attention to God's deepest desire for us personally, for the entire human family, and for all of creation. When we turn our attention in this direction, we find the scriptures pulsing with images that can inform us about God's will. The prophet Micah writes:

> They shall beat their swords into plowshares,
>   and their spears into pruning hooks;
>   nation shall not lift up sword against nation,
>   neither shall they learn war any more;
> but they shall all sit under their own vines and
>   under their own fig trees,
>   and no one shall make them afraid;
>   for the mouth of the LORD of hosts has spoken.
> —Micah 4:3-4

> *The Greek word* thelo *was used to translate the original Aramaic terms for divine will: "to purpose," . . . "to resolve," "to desire," . . . "to prefer". . . "to conceive."*
> —Nancy Reeves

The letter to the Ephesians declares that "[God] has made known to us the mystery of his will, according to his good pleasure that he set forth in Christ, as a plan for the fullness of time, to gather up all things in him, things in heaven and things on earth" (1:9-10). God's heart burns with desire that we all become one in the unity of Christ's love. God's deepest yearning is for shalom—the wholeness, harmony, and peace of all creation.

Moving to the most personal level of God's will for us, we have Jesus' straightforward statement in the Gospel of John: "I came that they may have life, and have it abundantly" (10:10). What is God's yearning for us all? That our lives overflow with goodness, becoming rich and full with the very life of God. (See Ephesians 3:19.)

Lifting up a further image of God's desire for us, Jesus declares that above all else, we are to seek God's kingdom or reign (Matt. 6:33). Jesus makes it plain that seeking the kingdom is anything but a private escape down some romanticized spiritual pathway. A genuine quest for the reign of God allows no withdrawal from the world's wounds. To live within this kingdom is to pour forth healing love lavishly, as Jesus did. It is to feed the hungry, clothe the naked, visit the sick and imprisoned, and welcome the stranger (Matt. 25:31-46). With this particular portrait of God's yearning, Jesus does not lay out a fixed map that we must follow step by anxious step. Rather, he paints a broad canvas of human need and invites us to add to that canvas with the brushstrokes of our love. According to our unique opportunities and gifts, we may create scenes as beautiful as a child cradled, a hand held, a hot hatred soothed, or an ancient injustice set aright.

Taken together, such images of the divine longing offer a vision of God's will that presents a clear direction for our lives and, at the same time, sets us free rather than constricts us. Contemporary counselor and teacher Thomas Hart observes:

> Where God's will is concerned, the analogy of good parents dealing with their children is illuminating. If parents love their children, they want life for them in the fullest possible measure. They want them to be mature, balanced, happy, free. They hope they will be discriminating, loving, bent on true value. They have not preconceived in much detail what will be good for their children. This they leave to the children themselves. Forming them as best they can, especially in their earlier years, they gradually give them more and more autonomy, allowing their choices to unfold naturally out of the developing sense of self.[3]

It is helpful to remember that the will of God is wholly consistent with the nature of God. That nature is perfect love (1 John 4:8). And in perfect, nurturing love, God wills that we grow both in experiencing and in offering forth the shalom, the wholeness, the very love that has given us life.

Love reaches out to the world through the branches of discernment.
—Nancy Reeves

Somehow . . . we have separated the will of God from God, and discernment has come to mean a search for God's will which we must find in a game of hide-and-seek.
—Rose Mary Dougherty

The Ultimate Intent of Discernment

Given God's will that you and I become ever more whole, and that we share this fullness of life with all that surrounds us, what is the intent of discernment? Many responses have emerged to this question. Yet, as with the will of God, they all point in a single direction.

Ignatius of Loyola, writing in the sixteenth century, clearly delineated the intent of discernment:

> In every good choice, as far as depends on us, our intention must be simple. I must consider only the end for which I am created, that is, for the praise of God our Lord and for the salvation of my soul. Hence, whatever I choose must help me to this end for which I am created.[4]

For Ignatius, discernment directs us toward far more than clarity on the immediate matter facing us. It holds in view the very purpose for which we have been given life. Through discernment we seek to live to the glory of God and to honor the redeeming work of Christ.

Writing in our own day, with somewhat different emphases, Thomas Hart speaks of the same all-embracing alignment of our lives with the purpose for which we have been created. He notes that discernment

> is not a magical formula for ferreting out the hidden plan, but a procedure for using our best human resources, in the context of prayerfulness and a life-orientation toward God, to frame and make those choices which seem most consonant with our selfhood and God's overarching purpose revealed in Christ.[5]

Profoundly challenging words on the aim of discernment come from Paul in his letter to the Christians at Rome:

> I appeal to you therefore, brothers and sisters, by the mercies of God, to present your bodies as a living sacrifice, holy and acceptable to God, which is your spiritual worship. Do not be conformed to this world, but be transformed by the renewing of your minds, so that you may discern what is the will of God—what is good and acceptable and perfect. (Romans 12:1-2)

Again, Paul writes to the faithful at Philippi:

The end of discernment [is] "finding God in all things" in order that we might love and serve God in all.

—Rose Mary Dougherty

This is my prayer, that your love may overflow more and more with knowledge and full insight to help you determine what is best, so that in the day of Christ you may be pure and blameless. (Philippians 1:9-10)

Here we stumble onto spirit-stretching matters! Our present-day sensibilities may cause us to blush. Me—holy? perfect?! pure and blameless? You've got to be kidding! Yet it is precisely at the point of our discomfort that the full intent of discernment breaks through. God wills something wholly fresh for our lives and for the world. We are to follow in Jesus' steps (1 Pet. 2:21). We are to put on the very mind of Christ (Phil. 2:5).

What, then, is the intent of discernment except to open us to the very fullness of life that God has offered us in and through Christ? We will never attain the fullness of Christ's life on this earth. But to align ourselves ever more closely with God's overarching purpose, to grow steadily in the world-healing ways of Jesus—that is the life-giving aim of discernment. That is what God dreams of and continually works to realize in all circumstances (Rom. 8:28).

*   *   *

As I think about the intent of discernment, my mind returns once more to the friend with whom I share coffee. Tom said, "I don't do it by myself." He also spoke those other words: "I pray." Discernment meant that much to him. It can to us as well. In an imperfect world, and out of an honest, questing faith, we, like Tom, want to open to the goodness God longs to give. "I pray." In the chapters that follow, we will explore many ways of prayerfully opening to God's leading.

Discerning God's will is living fully in the profoundly personal and fulfilling relationship … that God offers us in Jesus Christ.
—Danny Morris

Every opportunity to learn how to be more discerning calls attention to our radical dependence on the Spirit of God.
—Jeannette Bakke

DAILY EXERCISES

Read Week 2, "The Heart of Discernment," before doing these personal reflection exercises. Use your journal to record insights and questions, both as you read and as you move through these daily exercises. Receive this special time as a gift, inviting the Holy Spirit to guide and reveal what you need to perceive.

Exercise 1

Read John 10:1-15. Here Jesus uses several images of his role in relation to us: he is the sheep gate, the good shepherd who lays down his life for the sheep, the voice his sheep recognize. Each image reveals something of God's good intention toward us.

Ponder what Jesus' words and images tell us about God's will. Sketch in your journal a simple picture or symbol of each image. What character of the divine intention/desire do you see in each one? Note responses below your symbols.

As a "sheep," what do you find yourself searching and listening for? How does it feel to be searching and listening? When do you feel you have heard the shepherd's voice? What do other "sheep" you know seem to be seeking? Write a prayer expressing your responses.

Exercise 2

Read Matthew 28:1-8. In this resurrection account, the angel promises the disciples that Jesus "is going ahead of you to Galilee; there you will see him" (v. 7).

Thomas Green has said, "It is Jesus we discern and not just his doctrine."[6] How or when do you "discern Jesus" in your experience? What are the "Galilees" of your life—places where the risen Christ has met you? When have you "seen him"? How has he "gone ahead of you" to prepare for your arrival?

As you reflect on these experiences, what do you discern about God's desire for your life? Note responses in your journal.

EXERCISE 3

Read Matthew 18:10-14. Jesus makes it clear that he is saying something central about God's will in the parable of the lost sheep.

What does this passage tell you about God's deepest desire for you? What part of your life needs to be reminded of this good will? Write or draw your responses.

What does the parable say about God's deepest desire for those you cherish with all your heart? about those you find most difficult to understand or deal with? Write your responses in your journal. As you ponder God's good will, you might allow a hymn or song to come to mind and sing or hum it.

EXERCISE 4

Read Micah 4:1-4. This is the prophet's picture of God's great desire for all people.

Get this picture in your mind's eye. Let the various images of God's healing, restoring intentions play through your heart and soul.

If you were to paint a picture of God's will here, what would it look like, and who would be in it? Take your time imagining this. Let all the scenes and people that come into your reflection be gathered together. As you consider the whole picture, what are people doing? What are you doing? What feelings does the picture evoke in you? Depict in a simple sketch or describe in words what you see.

EXERCISE 5

Read Romans 12:2 and Philippians 1:9-10. These few verses speak powerfully of the particular characteristics Christians need to cultivate in order to discern and follow God's highest intentions for us.

First meditate on Romans 12:2.

- What does it mean to you *not* to "be conformed to this world"? List some specific ways this would apply to your current life.
- How do you understand the connection between being transformed by the mind of Christ and discerning the good will of God? Note your thoughts.

Now turn to Philippians 1:9-10. Ponder how love can shape your insight into "what is best." Then pray for the overflow of Christ's love and the transformation of your mind, so you can discern the way and will of God in your life. If further insights come, jot them down; they may be part of God's response to your prayer.

Week 3
Fruits as Touchstones

You will know them by their fruits.
Are grapes gathered from thorns, or figs from thistles?

—Matthew 7:16

Knowledge of ourselves and . . . our personal history of grace and temptation provide an essential background to present discernment opportunities.
—Jeannette Bakke

My eccentric, much-loved high school math teacher bounded into class every morning and posted a fresh quotation on the blackboard. We all knew the drill. By the time she finished writing and peered at us over the top of her glasses, we were to be copying the words diligently in our notebooks. She called these well-chosen bits of wisdom "touchstones." "You will never have to memorize them," she told us the first day of school. "What are touchstones? Well, touchstones mark things. They mark paths through the woods, swamps, EVEN OUR LIVES!" she said, stepping up her legendary volume. "THEY KEEP US FROM GETTING INTO MESSES. DO YOU HEAR THAT?!" Long pause. "Well, these touchstones are for your lives." Another long pause. "Keep them in mind." Here she cut back to a whisper. "Look at these touchstones from time to time. Check your lives against them. See how you are doing."

Then one morning, six months into the school year, our teacher broke with tradition. Right in the middle of putting up the day's quotation, she whipped around, glared at us, and said, "This one is really important. I want you to learn it by heart!" She had written the word KNOW. Then, in equally big letters and amid the percussive sound of chalk crashing against the blackboard, she hammered out YOURSELF, followed by three eighteen-inch exclamation points.

"That's lovely," she said, in a voice soft as mist. "Know yourself."

She stopped, arched an eyebrow, and scanned the entire class. "THAT'S IMPORTANT!" Then came a further hiatus while she gazed absentmind-edly at her desk and fiddled with her papers. "Now then, what are we supposed to study today?"

The next morning she pointed sharply at a girl in the front row. "Jan-ice, what were those words I wrote on the board yesterday?" Janice, who always knew everything, suffered an unprecedented lapse of memory. "Oh … well, it had something to do with … er … understanding who I am, and … uh …" Then, under a sudden rush of inspiration, Janice sat up straight, looked our teacher in the eye, and said, "You didn't tell us to *memorize* those words; you said learn them *by heart*. So I went home and thought about them, how they apply to my life, where I'm getting to understand who I am, where I'm lazy about it, how I can get mixed up if I don't understand what I'm here for, and …" Janice spent the next two minutes explaining how she had tried to learn the quotation by heart, even though she couldn't exactly remember it word for word.

"Good!" said our math teacher when she was done. "You know what touchstones are all about. TEST YOURSELVES. CLASS, HAVE YOU ALL GOT THAT? USE TOUCHSTONES TO SEE HOW YOUR LIVES ARE GOING. Janice, today you get an A+. But remember, that's just for today." Janice relaxed.

Touchstones. We need reference points in our lives—criteria, stan-dards to see how we are doing and where we are getting off course. We may use touchstones as they have long been applied in classical geology, where experts scrape precious-looking rocks against touchstones to see their true value. Is what appears to be gold really gold? Is what shines all silvery as magnificent as it looks? Perhaps, perhaps not. Test what glistens by checking it against the touchstone, and we will see the worth of what we are looking at.

This week and next we will consider two important touchstones for discernment. We will begin by looking at "Fruits." Next week we will turn to "Core Identity." Neither of these touchstones will provide us with quick and easy answers. When we apply them, we need to do so prayer-fully and with much personal reflection over time. If we act with care, though, each can open us to the guidance we seek.

Fruits: Anticipated and Assessed

In Jesus' teaching fruits emerge as a vital aid for discernment. "You will know them by their fruits," he says while counseling people on how to distinguish false prophets from true. "Are grapes gathered from thorns, or figs from thistles? In the same way, every good tree bears good fruit, but the bad tree bears bad fruit" (Matt. 7:16-17). Jesus speaks here in the manner of the wisdom teachers of Israel. He makes an absolutely commonsense observation based on the natural world: good trees yield good fruit, and bad trees do not. Like most wisdom teachings, Jesus' words reach far beyond the immediate context in which he spoke them. Considering the fruits can be a major aid in evaluating a whole range of life directions. In his final discourse with his disciples, Jesus makes clear that he is the vine and we are the branches. If we abide in him, we will bear much good fruit indeed (John 15:4-5).

> *We need to test confirmation of the discernment by noticing its fruits. What happens as we begin to act?*
>
> —Jeannette Bakke

How might we draw on fruits as a touchstone for discernment? "You can think about fruits in two ways," a retreat leader counseled a group of us some years ago. "Both are helpful. Sometimes you may use one, sometimes the other, and sometimes both." The leader went on to explain that we can consider *potential* fruits when anticipating the consequences of an action or decision. Might the fruits that come forth be good, fresh, and life-giving? Could they be harsh, bitter, or even destructive?

"And," the leader continued, "you can also consider the *actual* fruits when assessing the results of an action you or others have already taken. Here the fruits have started to grow right in front of you. Are they what you anticipated? Are they disappointing or even harmful? Or is the yield good? Is it giving birth to more life than you ever dreamed would arise?"

Of course when it comes to anticipating the results of an action, none of us possesses perfect foresight. Foreseeing consequences can be difficult. Sometimes, though, even the most general consideration of fruits provides the clarity we seek. A friend of mine had been mentally flirting with a harmful pattern for his life. I will skip the details except to say that the situation could have involved any of today's more popular ways of life coming apart: infidelity, experimenting with drugs, financial impropriety. Like many of us at some point on our personal journeys, the man was struggling, confused, curious, and attracted all at once. Nothing advanced his understanding until one day a mutual friend of ours confronted him with the words, "My heavens, can't you see the briar patch into which this is leading?" The fellow looked stunned. He said nothing. When we encountered him two weeks later, he had, with much prayerful consideration, chosen a different and decidedly more fruitful path.

Assessing fruits that have already started to grow poses its own challenges. Jesus counseled his followers to beware of wolves in sheep's clothing (Matt. 7:15) precisely because he knew that spotting the bad fruit of false prophets was not always an easy task. Nor, for that matter, is gauging the value of our own cherished actions. And yet if we watch prayerfully, carefully reviewing what is happening, clarity starts to come. This is true particularly if we bear in mind both inward and outward fruits.

The Inward and Outward Flourishing of Fruits

Sometimes the invitation to consider the fruits of our choices draws us into more subtle forms of assessment. Paul writes in his letter to the Galatians, "the fruit of the Spirit is love, joy, peace, patience, kindness, generosity, faithfulness, gentleness, and self-control" (5:22-23). Here the focus is neither on briar patches nor lush landscapes. The gaze turns inward. We are encouraged to view delicate movements taking place in the depths of our being. Paul's words encourage us to ask questions as precise as they are piercing: Am I growing in kindness? Am I increasing in generosity, gentleness, and self-control? Are joy and peace becoming more the hallmarks of my days?

Dag Hammarskjöld, the Swedish diplomat, entered a brief, heartfelt prayer in his spiritual journal the year he became secretary-general of the United Nations: "If only I may grow: firmer, simpler—quieter, warmer."[1] Amid all that swirled about him in the seething aftermath of World War II, the mounting pressures of the Cold War, the decidedly hot war in Korea, and the politically charged rejection of colonialism in Africa, Hammarskjöld measured his daily walk by how he grew within. Inward fruit was, for him, an essential touchstone.

Inward expressions of spiritual fruit generally become visible. The quieter, warmer person conveys quietness and warmth in even the most contentious settings. Patient, kind, and generous people radiate what is

Many voices call us: voices of culture, career, upbringing, worldview, peer pressure, ego, self-interest. . . . How can we distinguish between God's call and other calls?
—Suzanne Farnham et al.

Dear Jesus, help me to spread your fragrance everywhere I go.
—Mother Teresa

within them, often without saying a word. Here the outward appearance of inward fruits is subtle yet nonetheless perceptible.

Sometimes the outward manifestation of inner fruit takes shape in highly visible actions, bold words, and challenging patterns of behavior. Physician Paul Farmer, a man of persistent and gentle compassion, has devoted his career to the eradication of disease among the poor and forgotten of the earth. His life itself declares what is within him. So do his prophetic words, like the time he grumbled publicly over how much could be done for conditions in Haiti if only he could get his hands on the money that a small portion of the world spends on pet grooming.[2]

Those whose lives are barren of inward fruit also declare themselves, with or without words. Spiritual directors William Barry and William Connolly note that we rightly become suspicious "when the mystic can never take time to help wash the dishes."[3] Our inner substance, or lack of it, comes into the light of day, even if we are the last to see it.

Reflection on intimately connected inward and outward fruits can play a key role in our discernment. Often this happens on the most down-to-earth levels. Debbie felt flattered when asked to become president of an organization that reached out to immigrant families. She greatly valued what the group did and certainly deserved the honor. However, she began to consider what this additional responsibility would mean for her already overextended life. "I'll snap at my kids more. My patience will lie in complete tatters and, after three weeks of smiling while people congratulate me on my new role, all joy will pop out the window." Debbie declined the presidency.

Tonya received the next invitation to serve as the organization's president. She had the time. At least as important, she realized, "I'm learning so much about faithfulness and kindness from working with these families. These are exactly the lessons I need right now." She saw a chance to grow in spirit as she helped with an outreach that both she and Debbie treasured. Tonya said yes to the new leadership role. Debbie and Tonya had each considered the fruits. Each discerned faithfully.

When we adopt fruits as a touchstone for discernment, we finally come to examine our actions in the light of love. Writing about the fruit of the Spirit, Paul mentions love first (Gal. 5:22). In the final discourse with his closest followers, Jesus counsels, "By this everyone will know

Even when a need exists and we are well qualified to meet it, we are not necessarily called to respond to it. . . . To be doing what is good can be the greatest obstacle to doing something even better.

—Suzanne Farnham et al.

that you are my disciples, if you have love for one another" (John 13:35). The love we share with one another and with the world around us marks us as followers of Jesus. In love, the inward and outward fruits become completely one and visible to all. Patricia Loring, a contemporary Quaker, has called love "the ultimate gift or fruit of the Spirit. It enables reconciliation that binds up what is broken, joins what is separated and recreates our unity in and with God who is Love itself."[4]

When we consider whether our actions will bear the fruit of love, we grow in our sense of what radiates from our lives and stretches far beyond us. We ask: "What is my life giving forth to the world around me? By taking this action will I be following Jesus' teaching and example of love? If I continue on this path, will I be doing all I personally can to bind up what is broken, join what is separated, and recreate unity with God who is Love itself?" Such questions focus our search. They open us to the living Christ who, by the Spirit, continues to be our present teacher.

We are trying to choose a path that leads to goals consistent with the divine urge to love, and desire for healing, growth, justice, and freedom.

—Nancy Reeves

DAILY EXERCISES

Read Week 3, "Fruits as Touchstones," before beginning these reflection exercises. Use your journal to record insights and questions as you read the article and respond to each daily exercise. Enter the exercises in a spirit of receptivity to the revelation and grace of the Holy Spirit.

EXERCISE 1

Read Matthew 7:15-18. Jesus speaks here of how to distinguish between true and false prophets. Yet we could also apply his criteria to distinguishing between an authentic and an inauthentic Christian life, helpful and harmful decisions, or even between good and yet better choices.

Looking back on your life, when have you made life choices that led to "good fruit"—helping you to become more Christlike in some way, and clearly benefiting others?

When have you made life choices that led to "bad fruit"—taking you away from the love of Jesus, resulting in harmful consequences to you and/or others?

When you made these choices to go in one direction or another, what considerations were most important to you at the time, and why? Note insights or questions in your journal. Then pray about what you see in yourself.

EXERCISE 2

Read John 15:1-11. Jesus' invitation to his disciples here implies a connection between abiding in him and abiding in his love (vv. 4, 9).

Take time now simply to "abide in Christ." Don't try too hard to figure out what this means. Let the Spirit lead you into a time of quiet dwelling in the heart and mind of Jesus. Allow yourself to notice, to feel, to absorb what you find there.

Now bring to mind an important choice or decision you need to make—one you have struggled with or feel conflicted about. Consider this choice as you continue to dwell in the mind and heart of Christ. Which direction allows you to stay more connected to Jesus' love? Which choice feels more centered in the heart of Christ? Note any fresh insights in your journal and give thanks to God.

EXERCISE 3

Read Galatians 5:16-18, 22-26. Here Paul describes clearly the fruit of living by the Spirit. This passage can lead to a helpful form of self-examination, considering both the inward manifestation and outward expression of these fruits in your life.

List the fruits down one side of a journal page. At the top of the page, write *Inward* and *Outward*, drawing a line down the middle to create two columns. First note ways you sense growth within your own spirit in relation to each fruit. Ask yourself: Do I feel greater love in my heart toward certain persons? Am I aware of a new sense of joy or peace in my life? In what situations do I feel greater patience or self-control?

Then consider the outer manifestation of these fruits in your life. Write or draw symbolically how you see each fruit expressed in your life. Try to identify specific examples. Ask where friends, family members, or colleagues might see evidence of your growth in these fruits.

Pray in gratitude for how the Spirit is growing these fruits in you. Give thanks for settings and relationships that help you deepen this growth. Commit yourself to cultivate spiritual fruit, by God's grace. Then think of someone you know whose outward fruit of the Spirit you would like to affirm, and determine how to do so.

EXERCISE 4

Read Matthew 25:14-19. This parable speaks of the potential fruitfulness of using the "talents" given us, rather than hiding them.

Reflect on the talents you believe God has given you. List several in your journal. Consider when and how you have used one or more of these gifts well. Ask, "What blessing has come to me from using this gift? What blessing has come to others?" Write about where you have acted faithfully, and what fruit has come from it.

Now ask yourself if you have a talent you may be hiding. If so, what lies behind the hiding? Draw an image of what seems to block you. Let your reflections lead you into prayer—gratitude for gifts made fruitful through use, and petition for the healing of anxieties that may prevent you from using a gift for good.

EXERCISE 5

Read Luke 12:13-21. Jesus takes what we might consider a natural request for support in a cause of justice and turns it into a warning against greed for possessions.

What fruits of life do we lose when we are preoccupied with possessions? What do you think it means to be "rich toward God"? Jot down thoughts about these questions in your journal. Ponder how your responses relate to God's love for us and our love for God. Then consider how God's love relates to our discernment.

In a culture that stresses material wealth, how can you help yourself (and perhaps others) stay more attuned to the fruitful gifts of God? Pray to stay open to the abundant, life-giving riches of Christ as you face important choices in life.

Week 4
Core Identity as Touchstone

What are human beings that you are mindful of them,
*   mortals that you care for them?*
Yet you have made them a little lower than God,
*   and crowned them with glory and honor.*

                    —Psalm 8:4-5

This week we turn to a second major touchstone for discernment: our core identity. While any consideration of fruits, by its very nature, causes us to focus on what issues from our actions, core identity invites us to look directly at ourselves. Core identity puts us in touch with that foundational question, "Who am I?" In our culture, so preoccupied with image and outward appearances, core identity may be a hard concept to grasp. If we take the time to do so, however, we discover a powerful aid to discernment.

Know Yourself!!! my math teacher wrote on the chalkboard. She posted the injunction with every ounce of strength her compact body possessed. Yet the words she spoke next came softly. "That's lovely," she said. After all the years that have passed, the softness and loveliness echo in my mind. The phrase itself, she later told us, came from the Delphic oracle in ancient Greece. It has wafted across more than two millennia and kindled wondering wherever people have heard it. When we take seriously the invitation to know ourselves, we enter sacred space. "If you really know who you are, and if I really know who I am," my teacher had implied, "then we have a major touchstone for testing the direction of our lives."

In the quest for our core identity, we find ourselves inundated with differing perspectives. On a broad philosophical level, we may wonder if we are what some generalizations of humanity proclaim us to be. Are we mere beasts or crown jewels? Are we primarily citizens of the state or individual beings? Are we the proud masters of our fate or, ultimately, just a speck of nothing? Even as we form a response to such questions, we may sense that our answer has not pierced deeply enough to touch who we are in our uniqueness. And if we reflect personally on the question "Who am I?" we still find ourselves tossed about. Many of us have a well-developed sense of who we are, and others of us have at least a partial grasp of our life preferences, passions, and gifts. We may also have some inkling of how we appear to others and, if their perceptions are wise, this too can help. Still, as new opportunities arise, challenges stretch us, and life circumstances change, amid all that swirls around and churns within us, we yearn again to answer the question "Who am I?" On both broad and intimate levels, the issue of core identity admits no easy answers.

The Christian faith offers a distinctive perspective on our core identity. To understand it takes thought and prayerfulness. As we explore this perspective, though, we come to see that the Christian insight into our core identity is comprehensive. It embraces the broadest realms of our nature as human beings and, at the same time, honors the most intimate details of our uniqueness as individuals. Precisely because it values both the breadth and uniqueness of who we are, the Christian understanding of core identity can guide us toward fullness of life in times of discernment.

Who am I? . . .
Whoever I am,
Thou knowest,
O God, I am Thine!
—Dietrich Bonhoeffer

Beloved Child of God

Sometimes we use the Christian perspective on core identity without quite knowing we have done so. A number of years ago I was offered a new position in ministry. The position excited me, and I was flattered that others were giving me consideration. At the same time, I was not wholly sure. Something did not feel right. Then a friend helped me identify the source of my discomfort. She pointed out that I had spent my entire ministry in places calling for great emphasis on pastoral care and the nurture of intimate community. I realized that I served in these situations not because pastoral care and community nurture were more important than other forms of ministry, but simply because these settings fit how God made me. If I was to keep growing spiritually, I needed to honor the passions and gifts God had given me personally. Whoever went to the new position would surely do much good across the whole church, but in it I would starve for lack of community and pastoral bonds. This knowledge at least helped me understand my uneasiness.

Still, I could not bring myself to say, "No thank you." People I highly respected and valued expected me to jump at the opportunity. I continued to waffle until my friend gave me a further reminder. She helped me remember that God absolutely cherished me. I was God's beloved child. In this situation God's one desire was that I continue to mature in ways compatible with my genuine interests, abilities, and joys. With a sense of freedom and even thankfulness, I turned down the offer.

Unsettled inner feelings and the wise guidance of a friend brought me face-to-face with the Christian understanding of core identity, even though I could not fully name what was happening. As we grow in the way of discernment over time, the Christian faith offers a clear articulation of this identity. It is important for us to consider this articulation directly. From the start, Christianity has understood that we are beloved children of God (John 1:12; Gal. 3:26; 1 John 3:1). Our nature as beloved children is composed of two elements: (1) the foundational truth that we are loved by God, and (2) the reality of what we are becoming under the life-shaping power of this love. In the Gospels, mention of divine love comes first. Jesus makes it absolutely plain. We are all, without exception, persons infinitely loved by the all-seeking, all-embracing God. We are the very ones God came among not to condemn but to draw to life eternal (John 3:16-17). Each of us is the lamb that a shepherd risks all to rescue, the precious coin a woman turns the house upside down to find, the lost child a father welcomes home with overflowing joy (Luke 15). "Who am I?" we ask. "You are a person loved without limit by God!" comes the answer.

It is Christ's love for us that establishes the true self's reality.

—James Finley

From the reality of being so deeply loved arises the second element of our core identity: what we are becoming. We are loved so that, in the power of God's all-enfolding love, we may become fully restored in the divine image. Jesus himself is the image of God (Col. 1:15). If we follow in the way of life offered by him, we become renewed in the very image of our Creator (Col. 3:9-10). We catch strong hints of this when we consider the fruits of our actions. When our life path bears the fruit of love, we are surely growing to be more like Jesus. It is important, though, to see the full scope of what is happening here. Our life is not just about growing more patient, loving, just, and kind, as important as all these qualities are. The ultimate end for us is nothing less than restoration of all that God formed us to be.

Our identity as God's beloved children, then, embraces both who we are and who we are becoming. We are infinitely loved. We are, with all our vastly varied gifts, being renewed in the divine image, and we bear this image back into the world. We each do this in our own way—a thousand different ways, indeed a million ways and infinitely more. Our core identity comes with particular gifts. Unique gifts and graces are an expression of God's personal love for us, a confirmation of our belovedness. No two of us act, think, or serve alike. And God's love sets each one of us wholly free, free to be ourselves and free to be for others the image of the loving God.

Sadly, our core identity often gets snuffed out. In our culture we are frequently pressed to live not as beloved children of God but as children of the world's expectations. These expectations come from others, from society, and even from ourselves. In our early years we may hear unspoken messages from our parents: *Be the lawyer I never was, or the entertainer, the corporate leader, the celebrity.* As we grow, other voices can hook us. *Possess the big boat, the eye-catching car, the beautiful home. Raise outstandingly brilliant, responsible, talented kids.* We may buy into cultural compulsions of achievement: *Even though I detest where I work, I've got to rise to the top of my field!* Expectations take over, and we start to live pressured, anxious lives that bear little relation to the persons we truly are or to God's good will for us.

Ironically, living as children of the world's expectations can take over as the driving dynamic of church life as well. "Bigger is better!" "God's work never ends, so why should ours?" "More programs equal more activity on God's behalf, which equals greater faithfulness . . ." and as we follow such thinking, we exhaust ourselves. Our lives cry out for sabbath rest. Our collective spirit gasps for the fresh, life-giving breath of the Holy Spirit. Worldly expectations in our churches can crush our joy in service and cripple the vitality of the body of Christ.

Who I am must never be prostituted to the demands of what others tell me I must do.
—James Finley

When we do not live as beloved children of God but as children of the world's expectations, we ultimately wind up living someone else's life.[1] "I so wanted to be a teacher, but my father said, 'Be a minister.'" The pastor who shared this was fifty-nine years old. I ached at his words. "I wish we had the kind of programs you see at New Life Community Church," said the lay leader of a small, city congregation, speaking wistfully of the megachurch across town. The sorrow that breathed through her words lay not just in the tone of her voice, but even more in her failure to see the healing light her congregation shed by faithfully being present in its turbulent neighborhood. Living from the world's expectations robs us of the joy God longs to give. This immense loss makes all the more essential our staying grounded in the core identity we are given as beloved children of God.

Staying Grounded

To stay grounded in our core identity takes both time and prayer. Rose Mary Dougherty notes the importance of opening ourselves to the divine love that embraces us and works in the depths of our being to shape us anew. This means immersing ourselves in the images, thoughts, and reality of God's love. Such immersion may come as we pray with others, journal, meditate quietly on our own, or engage in some physical activity that nourishes both body and spirit. Whatever path we naturally follow, Dougherty observes that as we encounter the loving One who works within,

> our defenses and our images of ourselves are gradually chipped away; we begin to know ourselves for who we are in God—beings who are loved very much, who are invited to become who we really are, beings in love. From that place of core identity we want to make decisions compatible with who we are.[2]

Getting grounded in God's love is not just a one-time event. Our life circumstances change through the years. New gifts arise within us. Fresh opportunities beckon. Unexpected interests catch our attention and expand the horizons of our thought. No matter how old we become, the expectations of the world will still press upon us. In all these instances we need to get back in touch again with who we truly are. The need to

The ability to discern develops ... as one becomes rooted and grounded in the heart of God.
—Suzanne Farnham et al.

ground ourselves in our core identity does not stop when we reach a particular age or achieve some long-held goal.

Sometimes staying grounded means that we suffer. To remain rooted in who we are as beloved children of God, we periodically need to let go of what no longer fits us, and perhaps never did. We may have to endure the pain of releasing a job, a relationship, a cherished image of who we thought we were. Such changes often look frightening. In the face of both pain and fear, however, we need to ask, "Which will hurt more, making the change or continuing to try to be someone other than who I truly am?" Though the answer to this question may not take away the pain or anxiety, it can restore our perspective. It reminds us that staying grounded in our core identity as beloved children of God is, finally, about staying in touch with the deep joy God holds for us in Christ, the loving one into whose image we are slowly and uniquely growing.

Once I heard an old priest address the matter of how we can stay grounded in our core identity even when the choices are hard and we sense that faithfulness may lead us in difficult ways. He spoke to a group of us on a retreat I took shortly after declining the position that had, for a few days, looked so inviting. His words made sense. I can still see his smile as he spoke:

> Grow aware of where you feel most alive in God. What makes your toes tap and your life sing? Is it acting, teaching, or holding a hand? Is it standing for justice, working in a soup kitchen, or watching a child at play? Is it painting a scene, writing a poem? Remember when you were doing something and said, "Now I'm in the presence of God!"? Let that be your touchstone for everything else! There, in that experience, you knew that you were beloved by God and were becoming what God truly formed you to be. Let that experience be the measure that helps you decide.

The man said this a quarter century ago. His words remain as current and warm as the sunlight outside my window.

Discernment about what God desires does not follow a formula. It flows out of a relationship and personal history with God.

—Jeannette Bakke

DAILY EXERCISES

Read Week 4, "Core Identity as Touchstone," before doing these exercises. Use your journal to record responses to the article and daily exercises. Approach this time with an open heart, remembering how much God loves you.

EXERCISE 1

Read Luke 12:6-7 and 32. Jesus' gentle assurance in these passages comes, perhaps, with a twinkle in his eye: "Do not be afraid; you are of more value than many sparrows." Imagine the expression on Jesus' face as he speaks to his "little flock" about God's "good pleasure" in giving us the very best life conceivable, even the kingdom!

Dwell in these words. Let them speak to your fears—about your value, your worth, or how God feels toward you. Consider how much God cherishes you. Remember times when you felt God's love, joy, or forgiveness; the blessings of family, friends, and mentors; hard stretches when the Spirit has sustained you; ways you have seen, in Jesus' words and life, how much God cares for you; gifts and talents you have been given. Take time to simply rest in God's love, to absorb it deeply and receive it thankfully.

Then consider, "How can knowing myself as God's beloved child free and guide me in what I am living with this day?" Note thoughts in your journal.

EXERCISE 2

Read 1 John 3:1-3 and 2 Corinthians 5:17. These words speak of the spiritual fact that we are already children of God, and of the promise that we shall become yet more—more like God, shining with the image of our beloved Creator, Redeemer, and Sustainer. In Christ, everything becomes new!

What feelings rise in your spirit as you listen deeply to these words? What possibilities do you sense in the promise of what is yet to be revealed? Let images and thoughts arise, and simply take time to sit with them in wonder and joy.

Now ponder and list in your journal some old ways that are passing out of your life, and some new ways that are emerging in you. Then prayerfully consider this question: "What choices have I made, what paths have I followed that helped me to grow into these new ways?" Note insights in your journal, and close with a prayer of gratitude.

EXERCISE 3

Read Colossians 3:8-17. Paul offers here some very specific attitudes, dispositions, and behaviors to put off and to put on as we choose to be renewed more and more in the image of our Creator.

Reflect deeply on your life, asking: "What do I most need to put off, and what do I most need to put on, to grow into the divine image? How can I clothe myself in that love that binds us together in harmony? How do I allow the peace of Christ to rule my heart?"

Write a letter to Jesus, telling him what you think you need to become more like him. Ask him to reveal to you where you are on track or off base. Pray for his continued guidance as you grow in faithfulness.

EXERCISE 4

Read 1 Corinthians 12:4-11. In this passage Paul describes a great variety of ways people are gifted by God to serve the common good in the body of Christ.

Consider what unique gifts you have been given for serving the church and the world. There is no need to be shy about naming your gifts; in doing so you acknowledge and honor the Giver of all gifts. Name several gifts God has given you (they may or may not correspond to Paul's list in this passage, or to the talents you named in Exercise 4 last week). Write them down, adding any gifts others have said they see in you.

Notice the gifts that give you the most joy, satisfaction, and peace as you use them. How fully do you express these? Notice if you feel an inner tug to use a gift more fully. Ask the Spirit to show you a way forward, an open door for this gift. Then write a psalm or prayer expressing joy in all your gifts!

EXERCISE 5

Read Psalm 26:1-3. These verses speak of integrity, the testing of heart and mind, and faithfulness to God—all key in matters of discernment.

When have you made a decision or taken a path in life that felt truly right for you—that had integrity; fit your gifts; reflected your sense of God's purpose for your life; or just seemed right intellectually, morally, emotionally, and spiritually? Write about what made it good for you, and give thanks.

When have you taken a path in life that, at the time or in retrospect, didn't feel right to you—where you felt pressured by others' expectations to do something that didn't fit your best gifts, or otherwise felt off track? What have been the consequences? What have you learned from this about yourself? about God? Write your responses in your journal and give thanks for fresh insight. Pray to be faithful to God's purpose and design for your life.

Week 5

Growing in the Gift

George E. Day, ninety-four years old, handed me a small box wrapped in white tissue paper and tied with a blue ribbon. "For you!" he said on this day of no occasion in particular. "It's a surprise." His eyes glowed.

I carefully unwrapped the tissue, opened the box, and found a painting no more than five inches wide by three inches high. In that compact space, lush green hills rolled down to a shimmering lake. A distant stone church reflected pink rays from a low-lying sun. High, wispy clouds suggested early morning coolness. I stared at this unexpected treasure for a few moments, knowing that George painted in his "spare time."

"George, this is stunning," I said. "Do you paint often?"

"Every day," he answered. "That's the only way to keep growing in the gift." His eyes shone all the brighter.

I have cherished George's response as much as the painting. His words held not a whiff of vanity, just an honest assessment and steady determination. He had a great gift in his ability to paint. At ninety-four he wanted to grow in the gift. As we noted in Week 1, discernment is ultimately a gift God graciously offers to all of us. Whatever our age or experience, we can keep growing in this gift. In other words, we can always mature in our capacity to recognize and receive the gift of discernment, and continue to grow in our responsiveness to God's leading. We can, like my artist friend, become ever more sensitive to subtle signals that surround and beckon us. To keep us growing in receptivity and responsiveness to this gift, three pivotal aids are especially important: spiritual disciplines, questions, and willingness.

Spiritual Disciplines

Whether we enter the Christian faith as infants or adults, we soon find ourselves directed toward prayer, scripture study, and worship both in solitude and in community. As time passes, we learn of additional practices such as journaling, spiritual reading, and retreat. We could spend our whole lives exploring the richness of these disciplines. *The Way of Discernment* is part of a series of resources that help us enter more deeply into just such exploration. While we need not describe here all the sacred habits open to us, it is important to see how spiritual disciplines as a whole relate to discernment.

Our ability to discern is influenced by our willingness to observe.
—Jeannette A. Bakke

The monk Thomas Merton once asked an earnest student a question that he immediately answered himself: "How does an apple ripen? It just sits in the sun." The student, James Finley, thought long about that image and years later wrote, "A small green apple cannot ripen in one night by tightening all its muscles, squinting its eyes and tightening its jaw in order to find itself the next morning miraculously large, red, ripe and juicy." [1] The apple just sits in the sun. It is naturally positioned to receive the daily nourishment it needs to ripen. This is similar to how we mature in the fullness of God's life, except that we are not naturally positioned like the apple. We must place ourselves where we can receive the light of God, and this is the purpose of spiritual disciplines. Disciplines are regular, intentional practices—just like George Day's daily painting. Through them we position ourselves to receive the sunlight of God's grace.

Merton's image and Finley's response speak to the heart of the relationship between spiritual disciplines and discernment. As we engage in daily spiritual practices, we open ourselves to the Spirit's ongoing illumination. This affects us profoundly as we seek to live discerning lives. Sometimes we receive direct answers to the questions that burn within us. Sometimes we find ourselves sustained as we struggle to let go of our own designs and embrace God's deeper way. From day to day the experience shifts, but through it all God acts on us, the risen Christ shines, the Spirit ripens us for holy possibilities.

As we consider this relationship between disciplines and discernment, two spiritual practices especially call for our attention: questions and willingness.

Questions

Discerning persons make a habit of asking open, honest questions. They learn to cherish the value of deep questions, to pray and reflect on them over time, and to listen carefully for questions God may be asking them. With such questions they probe the issue before them, clarify what is happening within themselves, and anticipate possible outcomes. We have already caught hints of this. "What will be the fruits if I take this step?" "When am I most fully myself, most completely alive in God?" "Will this choice fit with who I really am as a beloved child of God?" Prayerful reflection on such questions heightens our sensitivity and leads to deeper understanding. It frees us to act faithfully with joy. Other questions can help us too.

Prayer, then, is the starting place of discernment as well as the atmosphere in which it happens.

—Rose Mary Dougherty

"I always ask myself, 'Will this be life-giving?'" The vibrant soul who voiced this question had faced an abundance of life's demands and pressing decisions. She went on to explain. "God is life-giving. If something will give life, then it is of God. If not, then I sense that I need to turn aside." She quickly added that the question did not always admit a swift answer. She often had to wrestle and search. Even so, she found that asking whether something was life-giving helped clarify the choice before her.

Many other considerations can help sharpen our vision as we seek the gift of discernment. Here are a few additional questions people have found enlightening:

• *How would this decision fit with the foundational teachings of the Christian faith?* "God never guides us to break divine law," writes activist Peace Pilgrim, "and if such a negative guidance comes to us we can be sure it is not from God."[2]

• *Does anything from my own particular Christian tradition, or from other Christian streams, speak to what I am considering here?* Many expressions of Christianity have traversed varied paths, developing rich stores of wisdom along the way. Orthodox, Roman Catholic, Reformed, Anabaptist, Methodist, Quaker, and Episcopalian Christians have all wrestled faithfully with issues of discernment. As we deal with particular questions concerning God's will for our lives, we can find much help in the teachings of these various traditions.

• *Will living out this decision or taking this new direction pull me away from spiritual practice?* If the path we are considering will leave us too preoccupied to continue nourishing our spirit, then surely it will do little to refashion us in the image of God.

• *Will this step strengthen or dilute the service I offer to others in God's name?* If we see that a new direction will only take what we have to share and spread it more thinly, we need to question the wisdom of that direction. If we see an enrichment of what we can offer, then we may rightly discern encouragement to continue.

• *What is my body telling me?* Our bodies are "fearfully and wonderfully made" (Ps.139:14) by God with their own hidden wisdom. For some of us, our bodies signal the health or toxicity of a path we are taking. A pain in the back may herald injury to our spirit. A knot in the stomach can speak of still greater constrictions in the soul. Conversely, the unexpected surge of energy, the sudden return of lightness in our stride, may speak the loudest *yes!* we will hear to our puzzling over whether to move in a particular direction.

When a choice has been made but not yet fully enacted, many find it helpful to ask, "Am I at peace about this decision?" The exploration of internal peace has a long history in the annals of discernment. Author Thomas Hart notes the deep correlation between Ignatius of Loyola and contemporary psychologist Carl Jung:

> For Ignatius, a choice in harmony with God's will brings peace; a choice out of harmony with God's will brings perturbation. For Jung, a choice in harmony with our true self brings peace and wholeness; a choice out of harmony with our true self produces anxiety and neurotic symptoms—headaches, ulcers, depression, guilt. . . . Peace tells us we have found [the fitting answer].[3]

The above questions are just examples. Some may be helpful in one situation, some in another. Still further questions will arise beyond these. The essential point is to develop the habit of exploration. Steady

To be a discerning person you need to be a praying person.
—Thomas H. Green

When we arrive at a clear discernment with logical and emotional congruence, we cease weighing options and notice we are at peace.
—Jeannette A. Bakke

probing will open us to God's leading. It will also strengthen within us an additional quality needed for growth as we follow the way of discernment—that of willingness.

Willingness

Willingness is a fundamental attitude of heart and mind. This attitude stands in sharp contrast to its opposite: willfulness. Willfulness says, "My way!" Willfulness sometimes locks its knees and refuses to budge. Other times it insists on marching full speed ahead when circumstances cry out for the need to halt and ask questions. Psychologist Gerald May notes that willfulness seeks "to master, direct, control, or otherwise manipulate existence."[4] It picks its own aims in life, takes charge, and won't let go.

Willingness, on the other hand, opens outward. Willingness accepts the simple truth that none of us possesses absolute clarity about the world in which we live or even about our own lives. It remains teachable and receptive. Willingness can relax locked knees and take an unexpected path when that appears the wiser thing to do. It can likewise cease all forward movement and ponder fresh alternatives, even if this means abandoning some long-planned journey. In its fullest Christian expression, willingness seeks constantly to follow not the hardened dictates of one's own ego but the supple guidance of the loving, life-restoring Spirit.

In scripture, willingness is an essential element in the lives of the faithful. When young Mary learns from the angel Gabriel that she will conceive and bear the Son of the Most High through the overshadowing of the Holy Spirit, she replies simply:

> Here am I, the servant of the Lord; Let it be with me according to your word. (Luke 1:38)

Above all, Mary desires to be open to the mystery of God's intention. She lays aside her own ideas and desires for the future. With a completely open heart, Mary offers herself to the fulfillment of God's will for her and all humankind.

The ultimate model for willingness is Mary's son Jesus. Early in the Gospel of Matthew he invites those who follow him to pray, "Your will

To pray means to open your hands before God. . . . accepting your existence with an increasing readiness, not as a possession to defend, but as a gift to receive.
—Henri Nouwen

be done, on earth as it is in heaven . . ." (Matt. 6:10). God's will, right here and right now, is to be the object of our fervent prayer. At the end of his life Jesus incarnates what he taught his disciples:

> And going a little farther, he threw himself on the ground and prayed, "My Father, if it is possible, let this cup pass from me; yet not what I want but what you want." . . . Again he went away for the second time and prayed, "My Father, if this cannot pass unless I drink it, your will be done." (Matthew 26:39, 42)

Jesus' agonized struggle in Gethsemane makes plain how demanding willingness can be. Willingness required that he let go of absolutely every-thing but utter trust in God. It asks precisely the same of us.

Even in less severe circumstances, willingness demands great atten-tiveness and sensitivity. Thomas Green compares the lives of faithful, willing persons to those who have mastered the difficult art of floating in water:

> The floater is not passive; one who is passive will sink, not float. At the same time, the activity of the floater is quite unlike that of the swimmer. The swimmer is in control of his or her own direction and speed, whereas the floater responds to, cooperates with the wind and the current. The floater's activity is a dynamic receptivity: God is the sea in which he or she floats.[5]

Not I,
but God in me.
—Dag Hammarskjöld

The floater does not say, "How can I maintain my course?" With all the senses of body, mind, and heart attuned, the floater asks, "Where am I being led?" As the answer emerges, often one barely perceptible nudge at a time, the floater follows. Responsive receptivity becomes the all-pervasive mode of operation. The floater—the discerner—knows that God is in the sea, and this person's one desire is to move with the sea.

I watched two such "floaters" some years ago. The demands of their journey, and the joy they ultimately found, remind me of what willing-ness is all about. For a quarter century this couple lived in a simple home that they took care of and loved. The husband taught junior high science. The wife worked for an agency focused on the needs of the poor. Yet despite being comfortably settled, they both began to feel a vague inner restlessness to do something different with their lives. Instead of ignor-ing the discomfort as so many of us do, they paid attention. For two long years they talked with each other, with friends, with persons they had never heard of before. They spoke and listened in prayer. At times all seemed calm; at other times, billows of uncertainty washed over them. Eventually a new shore beckoned from the horizon of their lives. As that shore took on specific shape, other clouds arose. I still remember the darkness one night when a group of us gathered with them. Tears. Quiet tears, and the flat, heavy words, "We'll have to let go of everything. All of you. Even the trillium in the spring."

A decade has passed since that night. As I write these paragraphs, seven thousand miles away in a district comprised of small, impoverished villages, this couple shares with others their ample skills and even deeper love. "I know it is a cliché," the man wrote, "but we are the ones who have been blessed, and amid the aching needs we see each day, our lives are filled to overflowing."

Willingness is about letting go of what we cling to and allowing God to draw us toward the greater life God yearns to give. Because doing this is difficult, we need the support of spiritual disciplines such as prayer, worship, and searching scripture for the Spirit's living address to us in the present moment. Yet the practice of willingness itself is a spiritual discipline, an attitude we can cultivate as a daily habit.

"Do you paint often?" I asked ninety-four-year-old George E. Day, so wise, so steady in pursuing his art, so open to how he might continue to learn. His gracious answer touched on something as rich as the painting I held in my hand. "Every day. That's the only way to keep growing in the gift."

No matter what method we use . . . the discernment process involves God's love and our willing responsiveness, surrender, and relinquishment of our perspectives in favor of God's.
—Jeannette A. Bakke

DAILY EXERCISES

Read Week 5, "Growing in the Gift," before doing these exercises. Continue to record responses to the article and daily exercises in your journal. Be aware that this daily practice is one of your own spiritual disciplines for now, and that by approaching it with a willing spirit, you position yourself to receive a discerning heart.

EXERCISE 1

Read Luke 9:18-20. Luke's Gospel portrays Jesus' questions to the disciples as growing directly out of his prayer. The questions we need to ask and live into often grow out of our prayer as well.

Consider your own relationship with God—especially in prayer, the root practice from which discernment comes. How have you been growing in this relationship lately? What two or three adjectives would you use to describe your prayer life right now? Note responses in your journal.

Think back to times you felt close to God or believe God clearly communicated with you. List ways you have sensed divine presence and guidance (such as through scripture, nature, dreams, persons, circumstances). Circle the ways that seem most natural to you. Give thanks for these avenues of communication, and pray that you will grow in sensitivity to them. Allow the Spirit to guide your continued prayer and see where it takes you. Notice whether any question seems to press itself upon your mind or heart.

EXERCISE 2

Read Psalm 119:97-105. This entire psalm extols the virtues of God's law (Torah), variously described as God's words, ordinances, commandments, decrees, and precepts. Notice the fruits or benefits the psalmist names from meditating on God's word, and ponder their relationship to discernment.

Reread verse 105. When and how has God's word illumined your own path in life? In your journal draw a path representing your life. List on/around it any Bible passages, wisdom sayings, or songs of faith that have guided you through the years. Has a scripture text ever become an unexpected "light to your path" in making an important decision? If so, mark it on your path. If a text has spoken recently to you for the first time, jot it down (just the meaning or essence of the passage if you can't recall the verses precisely).

Give thanks for any light given while attending to God's word, and pray that you will continue a regular discipline of listening to God in scripture.

EXERCISE 3

Read Philippians 2:12-13. These two verses contain a world of spiritual meaning. Salvation is a gift, but we must "work it out," living into the full promise of a Christlike life. Yet we can do this only because God is already at work in us, enabling us "both to will and to work for his good pleasure." Consider how this last phrase expresses the very essence of discerning God's will.

List three specific areas in your life where you feel a need to know God's will. It might help to ask, "What three questions do I most wish to find answers to as I seek to walk faithfully with God in my daily journey?" Write down what comes to you. If an image, diagram, or song comes to mind in relation to any question, draw or make note of it.

Give thanks for these questions and any clarity about them that may come over time. Pray to live lightly and steadily with each question, remaining open to holy illumination and trusting the grace of "God who is at work in you, enabling you both to will and to work for his good pleasure."

EXERCISE 4

Read Matthew 12:46-50. Jesus declares that those who do "the will of my Father in heaven" are his brothers and sisters and mother—his true spiritual family.

In your journal write these words: *People I see as true brothers, sisters, and mothers of Jesus.* Then prayerfully let come to mind people you have known or observed who lived not from willfulness but willingness, not clinging to their own way but opening their hearts to the divine will.

Write the name of each person you recognize as keeping faith with God's deepest and highest intentions for us.

Beside each name, write a sentence prayer of thanksgiving for the Spirit of grace that has worked in and through this person. Close with prayer that you too may follow the way of willingness, perhaps in very specific ways you are aware of being called to follow.

EXERCISE 5

Read Luke 1:35-38. These final verses of the Annunciation story speak to us of the spiritual dynamics of discernment. The Spirit comes upon us by grace at unexpected times, as it did upon Mary. How the Spirit works within us is a mystery, but if we remain open and yielded to it, what comes to birth is holy and in keeping with God's will.

Take Mary's word of response (v. 38) into your heart, and let it begin to express your own willingness before God. Turn one of its phrases into a simple prayer: "Here am I, the servant of the Lord." Or, "Let it be with me according to your word." (Brief sentence prayers like these are sometimes called "breath prayers.")

Pray this prayer for 10–15 minutes while you bring to mind each of the three questions or areas needing discernment that you named in Exercise 3. You may sit or walk as you pray. Then note any new insights or questions in your journal.

Week 6

In the Hard Places

Why are you cast down, O my soul,
and why are you disquieted within me?
Hope in God; for I shall again praise him,
my help and my God.
                                        —Psalm 42:5-6

*D*iscernment, we know, does not always come easily. Now and then we may swiftly see the way to follow, but often our progress toward clarity is more measured. On occasion the way of discernment leads to realms where we agonize. The task of seeing becomes long, laborious, even frightening. Our vision grows narrow, blurred, or utterly blocked. To bolster our flagging energy, we may tell ourselves repeatedly, "Discernment is a gift," but we open our hands and wait . . . and wait . . . and no gift comes.

Many years ago I heard a greatly respected pastor tell of his own struggle with discernment. His words caught me by surprise. For several decades he had labored faithfully in a rural region of severe poverty. There he helped build a flourishing ministry to address a great variety of needs: hunger, housing, health care, clothing, counseling. By the time I encountered him, the mission he led benefited persons from several hundred square miles of isolated forests and scrub farmland. I was young, idealistic, and serving my first pastorate. On impulse, I got in my car one morning and drove ten hours just to sit in his presence and learn whatever I could. Surely, I thought, this man had known what to do right from the start. As we talked that evening in the musty fellowship room of an old New England church, he turned our conversation in a direction I did not at all expect.

"The first years were harrowing. Economically, the region was a wreck," he said, naming a circumstance I knew well. Then he took the turn I had not anticipated. "Our work was getting nowhere, and I didn't even know if I was where God wanted me." He spoke softly, but poured every ounce of his massive frame into the nearly whispered words. "Finally one day I went out into a field and prayed, 'Please, God, give me a sign!'"

He paused here and looked toward the fading light outside.

"Do you know what answer I got to that prayer?" he continued.

I stayed silent.

"'No sign for you!' That's the answer I got."

The man rocked back in my direction, looked down at his hands, and settled into the quiet between us. Finally he spoke the words once more, "No sign!"

*   *   *

"No sign!" We may or may not hear a response as clear and dramatic as that. Yet we all have times when the way toward clarity grows torturous. We flounder about, grow tense with uncertainty, or simply stare into the unknown. The phrase "I give up!" crosses our minds, if not our lips. Or we start to wonder, *Perhaps I am supposed to give up. Maybe I have been following the wrong way all along.* At best we feel perplexed. At worst we find ourselves in deep darkness. *God, where are you in all of this? Are you here at all?*

No simple solutions arise for such times, no magic balm to ease our ache in the hard places of discernment. What we do have is the wise counsel of others who have gone before us through lonely stretches of wilderness searching. In the most practical, down-to-earth manner, their wisdom can aid us in those times when we must wait long and in those realms where we feel utterly desolate.

*Teach me the struggles of the soul to bear,
Teach me the patience of unanswered prayer.*
—George Croly

Waiting

Near the end of her book *Seven Spiritual Gifts of Waiting*, Holly Whitcomb offers the following observation:

> In God's time, we are often waiting for the bigger picture but must be
> content with each small piece. When we are waiting, we put one foot

in front of the other every morning and every evening. Waiting teaches us patience.[1]

Whitcomb's words rest on a key perspective offered by those who have faithfully walked the way of discernment: waiting, wherever and however we encounter it, can become a place of spiritual deepening. The waiting itself teaches us. Seasons when we must live suspended and unknowing can become crucial times for further formation in Christ. Waiting, understood this way, becomes an important spiritual practice.

Whitcomb ultimately names seven spiritual gifts that can come through waiting. Without claiming they are the only gifts of waiting, she offers them as invitations to greater attentiveness in our times of unwanted delay. For my own meditation, I have found it helpful to ponder quietly the gifts she has named:

Waiting presents us with a choice: To give in to the quagmire, or to give the quagmire up to prayer.
—Holly Whitcomb

- patience

- loss of control

- living in the present

- compassion

- gratitude

- humility

- trust in God

As I consider the list, I let the words rest there in front of me. I don't try to imbue them with any particular content or meaning. I simply wait on them, asking which speaks the quality I most lack right now and therefore most need. Is it indeed patience? Is it perhaps the willingness to relinquish control? Do I need to grow in the humility of acknowledging that I do not understand all things, or in compassion for others who struggle like me, or in gratitude for the many blessings I still have amid the uncertainties of my life? Answers to these questions declare themselves—occasionally to my surprise, sometimes to my momentary distress, but always to my illumination.

To note that waiting can become a place of spiritual formation does not mean it is pleasant, easy, or even caused by God so we can grow. It simply acknowledges that God is with us in the waiting, continuing to shape us in the most spirit-stretching delays. To acknowledge the soul-forming side of waiting helps us recognize that God may invite us into the gift of fallow time precisely to attune our spiritual ears. Waiting provides an open space in our lives where we may become more sensitive to God's beckonings and promises.

As we pass through times of feeling adrift, not knowing where we are going or what we are meant to do, we can learn from the rich biblical examples of those who literally floated at sea and had no idea what they were to do next.

Noah bobbed about on an oceanic flood, clueless as to when his ordeal would end (Gen. 7–8). All he could do was wait on God's timing. Eventually, over the long and landless days, waiting turned to watching. *Let's send out a dove,* he thought, and the dove was gone. *Ah. It's coming back! But what is this? It carries nothing. It has found nowhere to land.* Days passed. More waiting. *Let's send it out again.* A long watch until evening. Then finally, *Ah, here it comes with a leaf in its beak!* Noah watched. Amid the waiting, hope and a sense of future possibility emerged.

Paul and a half-starved shipload of travelers dodged shoals one stormy night off the coast of Malta (Acts 27). All they could do was wait in fear and uncertainty. Wait for the next ugly rock to slice out of the darkness. Wait for the nearly inevitable crunch and splintering of boards. Wait and, it turned out, do one other thing. At Paul's urging, they broke bread and gave thanks to God. It was a crazy, wild act. Wilder than the wind, crazier than the pitching of the boat. Their spirits lightened. They made it through the night. Dawn finally glowed crimson in the east. The ship itself shattered on a reef, yet all on board safely reached land, waiting and adrift no more.

At times we drift in our lives. Amid the uncertainty and suspense of not knowing, or the sheer tedium of things remaining the same, we can learn to keep our eyes wide open, scanning the horizon of our experience. Like Noah we may have to do this for a long time until at last some green sprig signals, "There's land ahead." Signs may beckon through something as ordinary as a phone call, as intimate as the touch of a child's hand, or as subtle as an inner urge whispering, "This is where you need to go!" Like Paul and his near-sinking boatload, we would be wise to feast ourselves again and again on signs of promise and hope even as we are tossed about on the sea of not knowing.[2]

Premature decisions are the leading cause of decision failure.
—Margaret Benefiel

Desolation … and Consolation

There may be times in our discerning, however, when we faithfully watch and absolutely nothing comes. We eagerly partake of the richest sacrament of grace, and it feels as void of nourishment as dust. Author Nancy Reeves notes that "everyone's spiritual journey involves wilderness or desert experiences, times when it seems that God has abandoned us. Nothing we can do gives us the sense that God cares, or is even present."[3] The inner voice of our spirit can echo the psalmist's despairing utterance:

> But I, O LORD, cry out to you;
>> in the morning my prayer comes before you.
> O LORD, why do you cast me off?
>> Why do you hide your face from me? (Psalm 88:13-14)

In discernment, resist the temptation to rush forward even when a matter seems properly concluded. … Put the matter to the test of the heart to see if it brings consolation or desolation.
—Danny Morris and Charles Olsen

Sorrowful, wondering, anguished, we find ourselves in the place of desolation. We feel forlorn in the fullest sense of that word: we feel lost.

In the midst of desolation a burning question arises: How can we live faithfully in this life-draining realm? Faithful persons venturing before us have found and offered answers to this question. No one answer stands alone. Each points to others, and together they suggest we can find still further answers. Among the most frequently offered responses are the following:

Don't rush to make changes. In seasons of desolation, change can take our minds off the bewilderment we feel. A fresh direction may hold out much promise. We need to be careful, though. Ignatius of Loyola strongly cautioned against rushing into change during times of spiritual desolation.[4] Contemporary grief counselors and pastoral guides do the same. New directions embraced too swiftly, particularly when we are in pain, may be founded on illusion rather than reality. When this is so, the change can leave us even more sorrowful and empty than we were before.

Talk with another faithful person. When we talk with a spiritual friend or guide about our desolation, we are no longer alone. Such a friend may offer a fresh perspective and, even more importantly, a loving, listening presence. Though our inner darkness may continue, we can feel that another's light has shone upon us.

Be open to professional counseling. God uses mental health professionals in the same manner that God uses nurses and physicians: for our healing. The line between desolation and clinical depression can be exceedingly fine, indeed at times virtually indistinguishable. If we find our emotions governed by feelings of cynicism, despair, and helplessness, we would be wise to seek a professional counselor who shares or understands our deep faith orientation.

Remain steady, open, and absolutely honest in our spiritual disciplines. "Across the whole breadth of your disciplined prayer life," a friend of mine counseled, "desolation will either break you down or break you open. The choice is yours." Desolation can break us down in one of two ways. It can snuff out our practices entirely. Discouraged or angry, we may simply quit trying to listen to God. Or desolation can drive us into a false piety where we go through the motions but attach no real meaning or hope to what we do.

On the other hand, we can let desolation break us wide open. Here we continue our discipline of looking to God while remaining rigorously faithful to what we are experiencing. Such faithfulness may include pouring out our anguish and wondering, sharing it as honestly as Job or the bewildered voice in Psalm 88. Like both these figures, as we offer our distress, we remain connected with the living God, open and ready to be formed anew in whatever way the Spirit chooses.

Know that the time of desolation will pass. "Weeping may linger for the night, but joy comes with the morning" (Ps. 30:5). The verses surrounding this insight make clear that their author had experienced deep distress. The psalmist had also learned a fundamental lesson: desolation will end; joy will return. Great Christian figures like John of the Cross and Ignatius of Loyola spoke of this same redemptive rhythm. So too did both my grandmothers, bless them, and a host of other faithful persons I have been privileged to watch over the years. In the darkest places we need to remind ourselves that dawn will follow—even as we strain our eyes and catch not the faintest glimmer of light.

Desolation is inextricably linked to this larger rhythm of the spirit. When he wrote of desolation, Ignatius named its opposite: consolation. Consolation is a time of deep solace for our souls. It comes on us as the season of comfort, the day of sensing the Holy Spirit, the hour

When one is in desolation, he should strive to persevere in patience.

—Ignatius of Loyola

of knowing the eternal, enfolding presence of the living God. Consolation is more than surface feelings of happiness or security. It is marked by a deep sense of rightness and peace.

Fully understood, consolation can serve as both a solace for our spirits and a guide for discernment. Several years ago I passed through much confusion and uncertainty about a choice I had made several months earlier. Heavyhearted, I turned to a professional counselor who I knew shared my faith. His words one afternoon illuminated for me the life-giving reality of consolation. "Do you remember, Steve, when you made this decision and were wholly at peace with God? Do you remember the deep rightness and joy you felt then? Steve, that sense of rightness and joy is where you were truly moored in God. You made the correct choice, but for now the way is hard. Let the memory of that faithful beginning sustain and guide you. Touch into it daily. And know that this time of turbulence will pass."

I felt adrift, wholly tossed about. This faithful professional pointed me back to my moorings. He reminded me of a fundamental sense of rightness more powerful than all my distress. I found much comfort in what he said. I also heard clear guidance. Faithfully remembered, seasons of consolation become touchstones for us—major sources of discernment when we must chart a course through the storms of adversity.

Both consolation and desolation can aid us when we look toward the future, seeking to discern whether a possible decision is of God or not. As we test the decision, we may ask: "How is it with my spirit? When I imagine myself living into this choice, do I inwardly sense desolation or consolation, oppressive clouds or the lightness of freedom?" Such questions can open us to God's leading in times of choice. And I have found they can aid us greatly when we need to renew our sense of why, in the midst of difficulty, we are following a particular path.

Not everyone experiences the wider extremes on the spectrum between desolation and consolation. The movement between confusion and clarity, between distress and peace, may feel moderate enough that terms like *desolation* and *consolation* seem somewhat dramatic or incongruent. Yet it is helpful to be aware of these common states of the human spirit. We cannot predict when an experience of true desolation

Consolation is when we feel energized, hopeful, and alive with godly contentment. . . . Desolation is when we feel our energy is sapped or that we are being drawn away from God.
—Jeannette Bakke

or consolation may occur, either in our own journey or those whose journeys we may accompany.

* * *

My respected pastor friend kept talking that night. He did not again refer to his prayer and God's response of "No sign!" Instead he told stories: stories of projects that worked out and others that failed; stories of lives that touched him deeply and circumstances that had nearly driven him crazy; stories of times he had thrashed about in the darkness, not knowing what to do. But through it all, even the wildest tales, his relaxed bearing offered something I carried with me on the long drive home the next day. Here was a person who, in the hardest places, had learned to wait, to keep going, to stay fixed on God, to be broken open and changed. His whole demeanor seemed to say, "God will provide. It may take a long time to see the way, but God will lead."

Looking back, I believe this trust in divine provision was the abiding consolation my friend depended upon to persevere through desolation. No external sign, but an inner sense of being on the right path sustained him. And, as often happens in the community of the faithful, his example has sustained me many times in my own desolation. As we continue to explore discernment, we will turn next to the whole community of the faithful.

All I know is that I have come to trust God more in my unknowing than I did in my knowing. I am not always comfortable in this place, but it's the only place I can be.
—Rose Mary Dougherty

Summation for Personal Discernment:
Prayerfully Drawing Matters Together

In chapters 3 through 6, we have considered a rich variety of ways to position ourselves to receive God's gift of discernment. Ultimately, there is no set path for receiving the gift, no single progression of steps that will bring us from seeking the gift to looking directly upon it. Yet many find it helpful to have a process they can prayerfully follow. Here is a simple one to try. If you choose to use it, do so with freedom. Take as long as you need in any one phase. Move back and forth between steps if you wish. If you find it helpful, take notes or journal your thoughts as you go along. Perhaps as you take just one particular step the gift will be right there for you. If so, rejoice and give thanks! Or perhaps you will find yourself led from one area of reflection to another and yet another. This too can be cause for gratitude; our loving God often draws us gently toward the understanding we seek as we are ready to receive it. Here then, to be taken lightly and freely, is a process for personal discernment that draws together what we have been learning:

1. *Begin in prayerful quiet.* Offer to God any particular cares or concerns you have. Pray for a willing spirit, fully open to God's yearning for you and your life. Take time to sense God's desire to lead you in ways that are life-giving.

2. *Clarify the matter you seek to discern.* State it as a question, knowing that at some point along the way part of your discernment may be a shift in the question itself.

3. *Consider the fruits.* Will following this choice help you grow in the fruit of the Spirit, or will it lead to less desirable outcomes in your life? If you have already begun to follow the direction you have chosen, are the emerging fruits helping you grow more in the image of Christ or turning you aside from such growth?

4. *Consider your core identity.* Are you drawn to this choice because it resonates with your deepest joys, your unique gifts, and your fundamental nature as a beloved child or God? Conversely, are

you in some way feeling pressured (or pressuring yourself) to live as a child of the world's expectations?

5. *Ask more questions!* Consider what might open you to divine illumination. Explore some of the following questions or others that come to you:

- Will this decision be life-giving? How, and to whom?
- How would this decision fit with foundational teachings of Christian faith?
- Will this step strengthen or dilute the service I can offer to God?
- How well does this direction fit what I am learning through my spiritual disciplines?
- Will this step pull me away from spiritual practice or draw me closer?
- What is my body telling me as I consider the alternatives before me?

6. *Test your choice,* prayerfully considering peace, desolation, and consolation. As your choice emerges, test it in the manner you find most helpful. You might ask, "Am I at peace about this decision, or simply relieved?" You might project yourself into the future and consider whether you sense consolation or desolation as you imagine taking this particular step.

7. *When clarity comes, move forward with confidence, joy, and thanksgiving to God,* for truly you have received a gift!

Be still, my soul . . .
All now mysterious shall
be bright at last.
—Katharina von Schlegel

DAILY EXERCISES

Read Week 6, "In the Hard Places," before reflecting on these exercises in the days that follow. Use your journal to record questions, insights, prayers, and sketches in response to the article and daily exercises. Recall God's grace frequently as you ponder the difficult places of life and faith.

EXERCISE 1

Read Psalm 130:5-7. The psalmist expresses an intense yearning for God's redeeming love in this prayer. Let yourself feel, as deeply as you can, this longing for God to come—a waiting in hope even greater than the desire of a night watchman to see dawn's first light after hours of darkness.

Select one of the three issues/questions you named in Week 5, Daily Exercise 3, or another matter where you are waiting for clear direction concerning God's desire. Keep this situation in mind now as you quietly ponder Holly Whitcomb's "seven gifts of waiting" listed on page 64 of this week's reading. Reflect in the way described in the paragraph following the list. Spend a few minutes with each word to see what speaks to you.

Note insights in your journal. Then pray to be alert to the gifts that are emerging or may arise in your current experience of waiting for clarity about the issue you have selected.

EXERCISE 2

Read Genesis 45:1-8. Joseph's insight in this scene with his brothers was many years in the making. Recall how his brothers betrayed and sold him to strangers. In Egypt, Joseph languished in servitude and prison, and then he rose to great heights but knew nothing of his family back home. Now, after decades, the divine intent through it all became clear: "God sent me before you to preserve life" (v. 5).

Looking back at your life, when have you discovered a larger purpose in long waiting? Recall your feelings as you waited, and name them in your journal. What was the gift in the waiting? Did something work out better than you could have imagined? Did you grow inwardly stronger or become more understanding and compassionate? Did the waiting turn out to provide much-needed rest?

Write a prayer of thanks to God for the gifts of waiting that you can identify in your life.

EXERCISE 3

Read Psalm 139:23-24. These two verses express the purpose and spirit of self-examination, or examen. The practice of examen begins with the cry, "Search me, O God, and know my heart," for only God knows us well enough to reveal us to ourselves.

Look back at the past twenty-four hours. Ask yourself these paired questions:

- Where was I most aware of God's presence? How was it with my soul in these moments?

- Where was I least aware of God's presence? How was it with my soul at those times?

Draw a symbolic picture of how it was with your soul in each case. Use crayons to draw, or write names of colors that correspond to your feelings. Then reflect on how these feelings help you become more aware of and responsive to God's reality in your daily life.

EXERCISE 4

Read Psalm 13. Like many psalms of lament, this one begins with a cry of distress, moves to an appeal for God's help, and concludes with words of deep trust and hope. The movement from desolation to consolation may seem unnaturally rapid, but likely the writer was condensing inner experiences that could take days or even months to resolve.

Read verses 1-4 again slowly. Let come to mind a time in your life when you cried out like this, or wanted to. Allow yourself to sense once again your distress and yearning for God's help. Rewrite or paraphrase these verses to fit your own circumstance.

Then read verses 5-6. Think of an occasion in your life when, after much turmoil, you could truly say, "God has dealt bountifully with me." Sense again the joy or relief of this graced time. Let your body express your joy through gesture and movement.

Journal your reflections on both the desolation and the consolation you have just recalled. Resolve that in desolation you will freely express in prayer what you feel, and that in consolation you will deeply savor the blessings and recall them in periods of desolation.

Exercise 5

Read Philippians 4:12-14. Paul is clearly touched and grateful for how the Philippians have reached out to him with prayer and concern. Writing out of the maturity of living for years with faith, he can also say truthfully and joyfully that he has learned to carry on through thick and thin: "I can do all things through [Christ] who strengthens me."

Consider prayerfully and note in your journal:

- In what areas have I already lived with the confidence that I can do what I need to do through Christ who strengthens me?

- Where am I still learning to trust more fully?

Pray in thanksgiving for the confidence in Christ that you already know, and pray to continue growing and maturing in the trust Paul shares in these verses. See if any song of faith comes to mind that expresses this trust, and if a verse or refrain comes to mind, let it help you carry your prayer into the day or into your dreams.

Week 7
Communal Discernment— Beginnings

Lead a life worthy of the calling to which you have been called, with all humility and gentleness, with patience, bearing with one another in love, making every effort to maintain the unity of the Spirit in the bond of peace. There is one body and one Spirit.

—Ephesians 4:1-4

I attended their spirited conference in the dual role of observer and member of the planning team. Thirty-three in number, they came from businesses, educational institutions, social service agencies, churches, and denominational organizations. They held two things in common. First, all were deeply committed Christians. In this fundamental matter they varied like wildflowers strewn on a hillside. The opening day I met Roman Catholics and Quakers, Episcopalians and Brethren, Methodists, Baptists, and Lutherans. "I'm from the United Church of Christ." "I'm a Presbyterian." I listened and kept adding to my mental list. Second, all shared a single passion: they were exploring how groups of Christians can discern God's will together. "In all our diverse communities of faith, how can we more clearly see the leading of God?" they asked. Communal discernment received their laserlike focus for three days.

As I listened to the group, I heard a delightful cacophony. No two people told the same story. Not one possessed the perfect method for discernment in community. It sounded as though some had no set method at all, just a "We tried this," followed by the tale of some spontaneous venture that ended in fresh learning. Yet beneath all the notes of their sharing, I could hear one steady, connecting tone: joy.

The process of spiritual discernment recognizes the gifts and insights of individuals. It also looks to the wisdom of the whole community.
—Danny Morris and Charles Olsen

The second evening of the conference, participants sat in a large circle. One by one they named the blessings they had received through communal discernment. Among the benefits they cited were these:

- Our relationships grow stronger.

- We sense God's power in fresh ways.

- Differences are honored and also transcended.

- We experience holy "aha's!"

- We see possibilities we never thought of before.

- We trust what comes forth and stay committed to it.

- The future looks hopeful.

The group was not naive. "Communal discernment takes deep commitment," one person said. "It presents no guaranteed method or quick and easy way to see God's will." Still, communal discernment was clearly an inviting prospect to this group. It held out the realistic hope of walking more closely with the living God in the shared work of various expressions of the family of Christ.

I have thought often about that conference. Many of us long for our communities of faith to walk more closely with God and to see God's will more clearly. We may experience this longing as we struggle with conflicting ideas of God's will in our congregations and denominations. We may ache as we contemplate the gap between Jesus' call for mutual love (John 13:35) and what we actually show the world with our competing visions of faithfulness. Or our yearning may have little to do with brokenness in the body of Christ. Excited and full of anticipation, we may seek to hear God's fresh call for our particular fellowship. "What is God inviting us to do now?" we ask. Parliamentary procedure, basic management skills, and conflict resolution techniques offer some help in our organizational life, but we can still sense an abiding need to open more completely to God's leading among us. Those exploring communal discernment tell us, "Look! Here is a way."

This week and next we will consider communal discernment. As became clear at that conference, discernment in community takes many forms. Three days could not contain them, nor can two chapters. What is both possible and exciting, though, is to see how this deep way of living together can become a gift to the whole church. This week we will consider basic beginnings: What is needed for communal discernment to flourish, and what are some simple steps we can take to enter the way of discernment in the life we share together? Next week we will explore going farther in embracing the gift of discernment in our common life.

Climate

"What climate predisposes groups to discernment, and how might we create such a climate?" a Quaker leader asked the conference. A Kansas resident, she knows climate makes a world of difference. What will the earth yield? What will come forth from a gathering of human lives? In each instance, climate is vital. This woman's question implied that while we can control neither the number of sunny spring days nor the amount of rainfall in August, we can nurture an environment in which people open themselves to receive the gift of discernment when God offers it in their common life. Many consider the following elements to be essential in fostering a healthy climate for communal discernment:

1. *The presence and practice of personal discernment.* "Corporate discernment assumes the practice of individual discernment by participating members."[1] Charles Olsen offers this perspective in his classic work *Transforming Church Boards into Communities of Spiritual Leaders.* As Olsen notes, this insight rests on four hundred years of experience with the teachings of Ignatius of Loyola. If a community seeks God's will together, its members must bring to the task their practice of, and passion for, attending to God's leading in their personal lives.

The structure of *The Way of Discernment* acknowledges the wisdom of the Ignatian tradition in this matter. While it leads us toward discernment in community with others, an essential element in the climate for such discernment is prior attention to our own practices of personal discernment, such as those we have been exploring through the preceding six weeks of this study.

2. *An abiding, shared trust in the leadership of the risen Christ.* As we become practiced in seeking God's will in our personal lives, we realize that the gift of discernment comes not through our efforts but from the

Cultivating receptivity with love will exercise our "listening" muscle, helping us to hear the divine more clearly.
—Nancy Reeves

Loving One who leads and sustains us in countless ways. I am still amazed at how easily I forget this truth when I enter into discerning with others. I am tempted to show how quickly I can come up with insights on what to do. Or I will have my pet idea that I *know* is right. Or I may simply want to leave my own little mark of an idea on the emerging vision so I can say, "There. That part of it was mine."

I would like to think I am alone in such faults. I have been in enough gatherings of the eagerly faithful to know I am not. And for some of us, when we don't give in to the temptation to push our own prized ideas, we can get hooked instead on the latest management tool we've heard of and convince ourselves that following one particular process will, at last, bring us out just where we need to be.

A healthy climate for communal discernment obliges us to set aside all such illusions. We need to relax and reach back to the fundamental lesson that lies at the root of our personal discernment. We can trust deeply, but not in ourselves or our prized methods. Rather we can trust wholly in the One who has promised that "where two or three are gathered in my name, I am there among them" (Matt. 18:20). In this way we encourage one another to recall that the leadership of the risen Lord is present, intimate, and available to the church right now, in real time.

3. *A growing trust in one another.* Mutual trust is essential for the flourishing of discernment. Such trust may not be present from the start, but when we take such vital steps as worshiping whenever we gather, sharing our faith stories, and praying for one another while apart, we come to see one another as followers of the same risen Lord, even while we may differ on certain matters dear to our hearts.

4. *A clear identity as part of the body of Christ in the world.* When we join with other Christians in seeking God's will together, we need to remind ourselves that we are called to be nothing less than a part of the body of Christ in the world (1 Cor. 12:27). Our unity in Christ is to be a precious sign to a fractured world. This means that our way of discerning God's current intentions for our community is to be marked by patient listening and graciousness toward one another. To fulfill our identity as Christ's body also means that we offer his healing love and justice to the needs that surround us. Both in how we treat one another

[We] need to trust God by being attentive to how the Holy Spirit is present in the midst of those gathered, and by having faith in God's willingness and power to transform the situation.
—Victoria Curtiss

and in how we move into the world, we are to be the flesh and blood agents of Jesus' all-embracing reconciliation (2 Cor. 5:18-19).

5. *Willingness.* When we seek to discern God's yearning for our community of faith, willingness is just as essential as in our times of personal discernment. Our collective desire is not to cling tightly to what we already have, but, like Abram and Sarai, to be led forward by God (Gen. 12:1-9). We do not sit about projecting what we would like to do next, but, like the disciples at Pentecost, we wait upon the Spirit and open ourselves fully to its leading (Acts 2).

Willingness in communal discernment calls not only for open minds and hearts but also for shared humility:

> It is important that the group cultivate an attitude of humility that flows from a conviction that each of us has limited vision, that even collectively we see but partially, that only God sees everything.[2]

When fully present, willingness creates a climate in which the entire body joins in looking to God. The prayer breathed by a willing faith community, spoken or unspoken, is this: "Not from us, Loving One, but from you shall our guidance come."

Basic Steps for Communities Seeking to Discern God's Will

Groups grow in the practice of discernment the same way individuals do, not all at once but bit by bit. When we understand this, the movement toward communal discernment appears less daunting and more natural. Here are simple, practical steps we can take in our communities of faith as we seek to open our shared life to God's gift of discernment. They are basic steps to seeking God's will for the group.

1. *Actively place God at the center of all deliberations.* At the start of their guide to corporate spiritual discernment, Valerie Isenhower and Judith Todd write, "Discernment begins with putting God in the center of everything that is done in the church, including decision making."[3] Several years ago I watched a woman embody this insight in a manner that made a world of difference. When she became chair of a church board, she modestly asked permission to make two changes. "I would like to light a candle and place it in the middle of our meeting space. And, if that's all right, I'd like to place an open Bible next to it. In all our discussions,

Discernment often depends on gifts that we do not have. We need one another's insights, resources, and prayer.

—Jeannette Bakke

the light and the sacred scriptures can remind us of the One whose way we are to seek in everything we deal with."

After a year the woman's term of service ended. The board voted unanimously to keep the Bible and candle. "When Kate asked to do this," one board member said with a chuckle, "I thought, 'Well, let her try it. It can't do any harm.' But, my heavens, this past year we've really come to see that as a group we're to seek God's way in everything we do." His words expressed how even the simplest visible signs of inner commitments can be significant aids on the path of discernment.

Other straightforward acts can help us hold God at the center of our deliberations. Some groups put a cross or bowl of water in their midst. Some invite one member to serve as a liturgist or spiritual guide, often rotating this role from one meeting to the next. This person shares brief readings or calls the group into silence at various points during its business so everyone can pause and open to the presence of the living God. For several years I have served on a board where one person is "keeper of the flame" and sits in quiet prayer as the group goes about its business. If the Spirit leads this person to speak, then another takes up the prayer. Such simple yet concrete acts as these draw us to seek God's way in all that we do.

> *The meeting for business is first and foremost a meeting for worship. In such a meeting the central question is neither "What is expedient?" nor "What is the group consensus?" but "What is the leading of Christ in our midst?"*
> —Paul Anderson

2. *Watch for and respond to the reign of Christ.* Theologian Gordon Smith notes that communal discernment focuses on two main elements:

- where and how the reign of Christ is breaking in upon us
- our response to the in-breaking of the reign[4]

Jesus awakens us to the nearness of this reign: "For, in fact," he says, "the kingdom of God is among you" (Luke 17:21). As a community of his followers, our fundamental task in discernment is to see where and how the new kingdom is already breaking forth and then discover how we are to respond.

"Where have we seen the reign of Christ breaking in since we last met?" The governing board of a small church agreed to ask this question at the start of each meeting for a period of nine months. Responses came slowly the first month. The second month, people had a little more to say. By the fifth month, their pastor told me, people were seeing Christ's reign breaking forth in workplaces, classrooms, the local food pantry

and grocery store, the health center, the senior citizens center, an attorney's office, and "Goodness," one person quipped, "even the church!" By the eighth month, board members were asking, "How does God want us to respond to all this?"

We need to open our eyes and ears. In a culture so fixed on the superficial, the negative, the sensational, and the tawdry, we need to be a people who look for the movements of God's grace and stand ready to follow where those movements lead. The question is so straightforward: "Where have we seen the reign of Christ since we last met?" Groups that dare ask it begin to move deeply into the way of communal discernment.

Models for Individuals Seeking to Discern God's Will in Groups

In addition to group discernment of God's desire for the community as a whole, groups can also help individuals discern the Spirit's leading in their personal lives. This practice is called group spiritual guidance. In group spiritual guidance the focus remains on an individual within the group and this person's journey with God. Thus, group spiritual guidance occupies a midpoint between personal discernment and communal discernment around a particular issue or emerging opportunity. Part 5 of the foundational *Companions in Christ* resource provides a rich introduction to ways we can experience spiritual guidance in groups.[5] Group spiritual guidance is an easily accessible practice for faith communities and smaller groups within congregations. As a bridge to the next chapter and further practices of communal discernment, two models of group spiritual guidance in particular merit attention:

The Shalem Institute model for group spiritual guidance—In this model, one participant serves as convener, one as presenter, and all in the group listen for the leading of the Holy Spirit. The roles rotate from meeting to meeting. The convener often starts with a reading. After a time of quiet, the convener asks that all listen prayerfully to the presenter and open themselves to what the Spirit is saying in and through this person's words. The presenter then shares an issue she is facing or a story of how God is acting in his life. When the presenter ends, the convener allows time for any questions of clarification. The group then returns

"I look at God, I look at you, and I keep on looking at God." . . . The group's task is to keep on looking at God for each person in the group.

—Rose Mary Dougherty

to prayerful silence. Once more, the convener speaks and asks that all share what they have been hearing of God's work and movement in this person's life. Then comes an intermingling of speaking, quiet, and dialogue with the presenter. At the end, the convener invites the group back into silence. There is no effort to get everything summed up or brought to a tidy conclusion. The emphasis, rather, is on opening together to the ongoing work and guidance of the living God.[6]

The Quaker Clearness Committee—The Clearness Committee can greatly aid an individual seeking to clarify a personal issue or dilemma. Typically the person seeking clarity writes down his or her situation and gives it to committee members before the meeting. When all gather, one serves as "clerk" or convener. After a time of silence, the focus person restates his or her situation. Persons on the committee make no statements; they simply ask caring, open questions to help the focus person move toward a more precise understanding of the matter at hand and of his or her faithful response to it.[7] Ultimately, those sharing in the work of a Clearness Committee are drawn into the foundational elements of communal discernment. Whether as a focus person, convener, or committee member, all grow together in mutual trust in the leading of the risen Christ among them and in willingness to follow the Loving One's lead.

Both of these models can become channels for the guidance of the living God. They can help us grow in the practice of placing God at the center of all we do together. As we place God at the center of our shared seeking, as we catch glimmers of the blessings that come when we dare to do this, we desire all the more to grow in ways of communal discernment such as those we will explore in the next chapter.

> *Through questioning, challenging, or simply being present in prayer, the other blows the dust from our eyes so that we might come to recognize the leading of God's Spirit within us.*
> —Rose Mary Dougherty

DAILY EXERCISES

Read Week 7, "Communal Discernment—Beginnings." In the days that follow, reflect on these spiritual exercises, using your journal to record responses to both the article and the exercises. Let your mind and heart turn toward the corporate dimension of discernment and the relationship between personal and communal practices of listening deeply to God's will.

EXERCISE 1

Read Acts 2:42. This single verse indicates how first-generation Christians continually placed God at the center of their common life. It lists four foundational means for doing so: the apostles' teachings, fellowship, "the breaking of bread" (Lord's Supper), and prayer. Imagine the early Christians devoting themselves to these practices and the fruit of this way of life in blessings, strength, and clarity of purpose!

Create a grid on a journal page as shown here.

	Personal	Family	Faith Community
CURRENT			
POTENTIAL			

First, reflect on any way you (individually or with others) already put God at the center of your awareness in each of these settings. Note what you observe on the top half of your grid.

Now enter a time of prayer and ask the Spirit to show you ways to place God more fully at the center of your life in each of these arenas. Note what comes to mind in the bottom half of your grid. Do you see any patterns emerging from the whole page?

EXERCISE 2

Read Ephesians 2:19-22. The author is speaking to Gentiles who were once outside the covenant with God, but now by the grace of Christ have been brought into the "household of God." Spiritually speaking, it is an image of intimate family connection.

Meditate on verses 21-22, allowing a picture to form in your mind. What might it look like to grow with other believers into "a holy temple in the Lord"? Envision your *Way of Discernment* group "built together spiritually into a dwelling place for God." How do you already experience this spiritual reality taking shape among you? Note thoughts in your journal.

Use a pen, crayons, or colored pencils to sketch a symbolic picture of what you have seen in your mind's eye. Ponder this image and let it lead you into prayer for your group and for your church.

EXERCISE 3

Read Romans 12:2-5. This passage suggests that in order to "discern what is the will of God," we need grace to see ourselves clearly, with "sober judgment." Authentic humility means seeing ourselves neither more highly nor less highly than is true.

Ponder particular gifts God has given you and each member of your *Way of Discernment* group. Write in your journal at least one gift you perceive God has given each person in your small group. Then name one or two gifts God has given you, and one or two limitations you see in yourself.

Pray for the Spirit's illumination as you reflect on the phrase: "we, who are many, are one body in Christ, and individually we are members one of another." How does this spiritual truth affect your understanding of group discernment? Note any insights in your journal.

EXERCISE 4

Read 1 Corinthians 12:27-28 and Ephesians 1:22-23. First Corinthians emphasizes that with all our different gifts we are still part of one integrated body of Christ. Ephesians stresses Christ as head of the church, wonderfully filling his body and all things.

Take time to sit quietly with these images. Call to mind your friends in Christ—those you know now and have known through the years. See all of them, and yourself, as part of Christ's body. Then behold Christ as head and leader of his body. See Christ in all of you together, one body with his Spirit. Rest prayerfully with this image.

Now ask, "If we allow Christ to be our head, and truly let him fill us with his Spirit, what might he lead us to do?" Write in your journal what comes to mind. Offer thanksgiving for insights received.

EXERCISE 5

Read Luke 17:20-21. Jesus boldly declares that the divine kingdom—the reign of God—is already among and within us if only we would recognize it. It breaks into our consciousness when our spiritual eyes open to its reality—perhaps in the wonder of a child, the courage of one who suffers for the sake of truth, a sudden deep insight, or an unexpected feeling of compassion for someone hard to love.

Prayerfully ask yourself: "In the last twenty-four hours, where have I seen or sensed the kingdom of God breaking in?" Let thoughts or images arise, and note or draw what comes to mind.

Then ponder this question: "How am I or my faith community being invited to respond to this in-breaking of Jesus' reign?" Again, write your thoughts or sketch your images. Give thanks for new insights and pray that you will act on any invitation you are hearing.

Week 8

Communal Discernment— Going Farther

*Do you not know that you are God's temple
and that God's Spirit dwells in you?*
— 1 Corinthians 3:16*

*In this verse the Greek word for *you* is plural.

> *If the church has only one approach for conducting meetings, can it receive a vision, respond to an answered prayer, determine the highest calling, or ascertain an ultimate purpose?*
> —Danny Morris and Charles Olsen

O nce we begin exploring the gift of discernment in our faith communities, we naturally desire to go farther. If with simple symbolic acts we place God at the center of our deliberations, we quickly wonder, *Where might we be led if we really give God a chance?* If we encounter the graciousness and wisdom that come to an individual through group spiritual guidance, we soon ask, "Are there further patterns that can help us discern God's guidance in the lives of our faith communities?" The answer is, "Most certainly. There are many additional ways to open to God's leading in the life we share." What follows are three different approaches for moving more deeply into communal discernment. They represent just a few of the means available to us. Ways of discerning God's will together are currently emerging with freshness and abundance, as was evident at the three-day conference on communal discernment mentioned in chapter 7. I share these specific approaches partly because I have found each to be exciting and fruitful, and partly because their very diversity suggests the profusion of ways we can open to the gift of discernment God longs to give.

Asking a Long-Term Question

Six and a half weeks into my work at the first church I served as minister, I asked a question that could only have come from someone straight out of seminary and utterly lacking in life experience. I was a suburban kid serving in farm country. The question came to me the very day I was invited there as pastor. I had written it down and even rehearsed it so that I would say it precisely the way I wanted to. I picked what I knew would be the perfect time: my initial meeting with the official church board. Halfway through the meeting there was a bit of a lull, and sensing the moment had arrived, I ventured forth:

"Tell me," I said, sitting up extra straight and sounding as bright as possible, "what are the ethical issues in agriculture?"

My effort did not produce a big response. A couple of folks looked down thoughtfully, perhaps trying to stifle a grin. At least one raised her eyebrows, then quickly lowered them.

Better rephrase that, I thought. I took a second run at it: "What are the moral issues in farming?"

I should indicate at this point that I sat between Ray and Minnie. Together they represented forty-five years of farm experience. Ray, a gentle spirit who loved every animal ever born on his farm, responded first in his slow, soft voice. "Moral issues? Oh, well, I really don't think there are any moral issues in farming."

Minnie, full of energy, didn't let two seconds go by. "What do you mean by that, Ray? You know darned well that 95 percent of what we do is immoral!"

At this, everybody had a good laugh. Having no idea what to do next, I hurried us along to a discussion of the paint that was peeling off the side of the church.

When the board met one month later, several members had been thinking. "About those moral issues in farming," one farm loan officer said, "I've got some ideas." He named a few issues. Others chimed in, not on issues but on the question itself. "Pastor, couldn't we phrase the question a little differently than you did last month?" They spent a lot of time that night talking about how they wanted to word the question. A month later they spent more time on the question, and finally came up with, "As people involved with farming in a great variety of ways, what is God asking us to do to share God's justice and love?" Then they made a commitment that to this day delights and stuns me. They said that for the next two years they would encourage the entire congregation to deal with this

Prayerfully formulated questions invite the movement of God's Spirit.... Questions stimulate further listening.

—Suzanne Farnham et al.

question. Whether people were farmers, loan officers, government agents, farm equipment dealers, 4-H advisers, or parents of kids growing up on farms, they all would have opportunities to ask this question and to pursue it in small groups.

At the end of two years the board said, "We're getting somewhere but need more time." They requested another two years. At the end of the fourth year, the congregation produced an eighty-page report that dealt with numerous realms where persons heard God calling them to faithful lives as Christians involved with farming. Among the areas they considered were: the treatment of labor, care for the land, the use and abuse of government programs, loan practices, sound and dishonest practices in the selling of farm equipment, hostile and healthful relationships between competing farm organizations, and personal outreach to rural persons who had no previous relationship with the church. The report received wide circulation.[1] More important, members of the congregation acted courageously on the ways of faithfulness they had discerned.

"An unanswered question is a fine traveling companion," says writer Rachel Naomi Remen. "It sharpens your eye for the road."[2] The leaders and members of that congregation adopted a question as their long-term traveling companion. Their extended inquiry became a major channel for discernment. More specifically, their actions suggest a pattern that we can follow in a variety of church settings:

- Start with an initial question. Take time to refine it, making sure the question states clearly what we, as faithful people, wish to explore.

- Rather than rush to a conclusion, live with the question for an extended time. Address it in a variety of settings such as adult classes, women's and men's groups, Bible studies, and small groups. Grow familiar with the many ways God may be urging our responses.

- Set specific periods to review prayerfully the emerging answers. If after a review people say, "We need more time; we're not there yet," gladly take the time!

- Make a written statement of the answers that have emerged, give thanks, and encourage one another in faithfully living the answers.

In the process of spiritual discernment, the group patiently and prayerfully listens, struggling to see where the Spirit rests.
—Danny Morris and Charles Olsen

It is possible to work variations on this pattern. When government services to the poor were cut severely in my home state of Michigan, Roman Catholic Bishop Kenneth Untener asked that all committees in his diocese of Saginaw begin every meeting with one question: "How is this meeting going to help the poor?" Hundreds of people asked that question. It sharpened their sight between meetings and focused their thoughts every time they gathered. Over time, scores of committees discerned specific ways they could respond to God's call to serve the poor and forgotten.

Seasoning with Images and Silence

"A pinch of sweet basil and a dash of curry can turn even a baked zucchini into something worth eating," a friend of mine once quipped. For him, seasoning made all the difference. The same holds true for fostering a listening heart in group deliberations and discernment. Communal discernment can draw us into what at first seem to be long recipes of important steps to take, with various ingredients of thought and prayer to stir together. At times, though, we can season our deliberations with tiny, simple acts that yield feasts of insight we never dreamed lay so close at hand. I will mention two seasonings for group deliberations here: images and hallowed silence. Each is important by itself. Together they may help us grow sensitive to other ways we can flavor and enrich times of discerning God's will together.

Images—The third morning of that conference on communal discernment, our planning team found itself in trouble. After receiving two days of input from participants, we now had only forty minutes to synthesize twenty-four pages of newsprint and come up with pertinent discussion topics for the final day. We gave this task our best effort, straining to name the multitude of logical connections and emerging themes we could see. As the minutes ticked by, we felt increasingly overwhelmed. At least one of us (me!) was growing dispirited and crabby.

Seeing the downward spiral of our entire team, one member suggested we take another direction. "Let's stop trying so hard. Let's just be still, look over the newsprint, and see if an image comes to us that expresses what we hear God saying in all of this." We welcomed the invitation. For

The movement of God's Spirit cannot be predicted or packaged. Nor can any systematic method guarantee group unanimity at the deepest level. However, there are spiritual practices that can enable us to be more receptive and attentive to God and one another and help us discern the mind of Christ.
—Victoria Curtiss

three, four, five minutes we were silent. Then one member of the group spoke of an image that had come to him. It was as outlandish as it was unexpected, having something to do with fungus, beetles, and new growth. Even he did not know quite what it meant. We laughed, accepted the image as a gift, and took it to the thirty participants. They laughed, then spent the next several hours in three groups exploring communal discernment as related to fungi (all the odd and unexpected things that spring up when people discern in community), beetles (the ways God works with the fungus), and new growth (the vitality that bursts forth when we open to God in our life together). Two days of discussion, twenty-four pages of newsprint, and God's persistent underlying call had all found their way into that image. What began in confusion turned into the most insight-graced day of the conference.

Hallowed silence—Sometimes simple silence, hallowed by our yearning for divine guidance, is all the seasoning our group deliberations need. Many years ago a voice on the other end of the phone told me I had not been selected for a position that he and several others had interviewed me for earlier in the week. The man spoke with such kindness that I honestly felt no pain. What moved me most, though, came through his follow-up explanation.

> *The silence of prayerful listening is not so much the absence of talk as it is presence to the Word.*
> —Suzanne Farnham et al.

"We were absolutely divided between you and the other candidate. Some wanted to invite you to the position. Some wanted just as much to invite the other. We were getting nowhere. Finally we decided to enter into silence. We opened the chapel. Several went there to pray. Others went outside and walked prayerfully in the woods. When we came back together, we voted again. Unanimously we chose the other person." What this wise group had discovered was richly flavored with God's guidance for all of us, including me.

Pepper. Dill. Mint. Add them to the mix, and they will lift a meal to a whole new level. It is the same in discernment. Particularly when nothing blends together, we can spontaneously draw in the simplest ingredients: rest in quietness; open up to images; let thoughts of scripture or special words of faith arise. I have seen this dynamic now more times than I can number: when groups season their deliberations with simple acts of turning to God in fresh ways, they find themselves richly fed by God's presence and lifted to new levels of energy and vision.

Opening to the Gift of Discernment in Highly Complex Situations

Sometimes in communal discernment we must deal with highly complex issues. Feelings run strong. Conflict is often present. Yet even when it is not, we still need to pass through many levels of understanding before we reach clarity. We may face questions as immediate and vital as, "What is God's call for our church right now? What is God giving us to do?" We may struggle with any one of several broad-scope issues that in recent years have divided congregations and whole denominations. Either way, we perceive that God's gift of discernment will need to come over a long period, one step at a time.

One step at a time. That, for the most part, is exactly how the gift of discernment emerges in highly complex situations. A congregation I have long admired recently initiated a comprehensive mission program for all aspects of its life. This community of faith spent three full years catching its fresh vision. In another equally challenging arena, a group of twenty-two committed laypeople and pastors sought over the course of four years to discern God's will on some of the most complex issues facing my denomination. Initially the twenty-two were deeply divided among themselves. After a long process of opening to God's gift of discernment, those persons spoke to the wider church with courage, faithfulness, and a united voice. "Only the Holy Spirit could have brought us to that place," one of them told me.

One step at a time. These steps come in a general order, but never rigidly so. The movement is free, with the whole group sometimes shifting back and forth between steps, sometimes going around in circles. The venture looks more like a polka or ballet than a straight march forward. Nonetheless, there is a graced progression to this dance where the sole desire—and the shared desire of souls—is to become pliable enough for God to lead us where we need to go. Key steps include these:[3]

1. *Scripture study*—Groups seeking to discern God's will in complex situations wisely begin by rooting themselves in scripture, particularly passages that speak of God's call, presence, and yearning to unite all things in Christ.

Time constraints may lead busy people to rush to premature judgments.

—Danny Morris
and Charles Olsen

A leader practicing spiritual discernment needs to exercise patience in allowing different viewpoints and underlying issues to surface.

—Margaret Benefiel

91

2. *Faith sharing*—The group will grow in openness to God and closeness with one another as members share their own faith stories. Faith sharing will deepen the bonds of mutual trust that are crucial to facilitating group discernment.

3. *Prayer*—Prayer needs to be the constant accompaniment to this dance of communal discernment. In this regard it will be particularly helpful for the group to discuss regularly what it wishes to pray for both during and between meetings.

4. *Clarifying the question*—The group will need to give prayerful time to stating clearly the issue before it. Once the issue is named, the specific question for discernment can be tentatively stated, prayerfully reflected on, refined, and brought to clarity.

5. *Shedding*—Individually and together the group will need to shed preconceived notions and ready-made conclusions. This is among the most difficult steps in communal discernment, yet it is also among the most freeing. When persons name their previous attachments and prayerfully seek to lay them aside, they truly open to the leading of the living God.

6. *Gathering*—It is vital to gather input on the issue at hand from a wide variety of sources: scripture, church teachings, the diverse experiences and insights of faithful persons, and formal studies pertaining to the issue.[4]

7. *Prayerfully sifting*—The group will need to spend extensive time sifting and sorting all it has received. This step calls for deep, prayerful listening to one another and for what God is beginning to say through what has come forth.

8. *Speaking and testing the vision*—In time, group members will begin to speak the new vision of where God is now leading. With prayer and honesty the group will need to test what is emerging. It might ask: As we tentatively hold the direction we are glimpsing ahead, are we graced with genuine peace or just a sense of relief? Are some important elements or voices being left out? What fruits can we see as we consider this?

Too often decisions are short-circuited because leaders fail to ask what information is needed, or they fail to gather all the necessary information.
—Margaret Benefiel

9. *Stating the discerned vision*—Testing the vision may continue for an extended time, but when at last the vision of God's leading comes clear, it is time to state what has been discerned for all to hear and to embrace.

10. *Giving thanks and going forth*—Finally it is time to celebrate God's gracious guidance, give thanks for the gift, and follow the lead!

So we go forth. And the more we follow God's lead in our communities of faith, the more we realize that communal discernment is a never-ending dance. God leads and we follow; then God leads again and again. In time we come to see that in community, as in our personal lives, discernment is not just about making a particular decision. It is about entering into a whole new lifestyle of faith, a way of being constantly with God. Bearing this constancy of divine relationship in mind, our final two weeks will help us consider how, both personally and corporately, we are perpetually challenged and sustained as we journey in the way of discernment.

Every experience [with communal discernment] has always led us to a conclusion that none of us anticipated.

—John Anderson

DAILY EXERCISES

Read Week 8, "Communal Discernment—Going Farther." Keep your journal at hand to record feelings, insights, memories, and questions as you read the article and complete an exercise each day following. Continue to dwell on God's purpose for your *Companions* group and your larger faith community, allowing the Spirit to be your guide.

EXERCISE 1

Read Deuteronomy 30:11-14. These words speak not only to the newly forming people of Israel but to the whole community of faith across all generations. Here we receive God's simple yet profound promise that all the wisdom we yearn for, all the guidance we seek in life is, in fact, close at hand—within our own hearts to uncover.

Reflect on the phrase "the word is very near to you; it is in your mouth and in your heart for you to observe." Ponder the truth of this gift God has placed well within our reach, deep within us. When, in the past week or so, have you personally found divine guidance close at hand? When have you sensed God's wisdom "very near" for your small group or larger faith community? How has this guidance come? Note responses to these questions in your journal.

If you have time, take up a question or decision you are seeking wisdom for, and enter into prayer. Trust that the guidance you seek is very near to you, and open your mind to receive what your heart can reveal. Relax into the silence. Allow God's wisdom within you to begin to surface. Capture what comes to light in words or pictures.

EXERCISE 2

Read 1 Corinthians 3:6-9. The overarching metaphor Paul draws on in this passage is that of a field, sown and watered for growth only God can give. The field refers to the church in Corinth, but it could apply to any church or faith community.

Meditate on the image of a field, allowing various pictures or memories to come to mind. Envision your church or *Way of Discernment* group as "God's field," perhaps a plot within a larger field. How cultivated does it look? What stage of growth is it in? Is your "field" producing food or flowers?

Take pen, crayons, or colored pencils and playfully draw your image of this field in your journal. Color and label parts of it to depict "soil," "seed," and whatever growth or "harvest" you see coming from it. Offer your picture to God and give thanks for any fresh insight this image brings concerning your group or your church.

EXERCISE 3

Read Isaiah 30:15. God's word here is addressing "a rebellious people" who have put their "trust in oppression and deceit" (vv. 9, 12). Quiet trust in God's way rather than our own forceful efforts to gain and maintain control is a consistent theme in scripture.

The author suggests that the same is true when we have trouble finding our way forward in discernment. He offers this simple counsel: "rest in quietness; open up to images; let thoughts of scripture or special words of faith arise." Try this exercise in listening to God:

Compose yourself in quiet: relax, breathe deeply, and re-collect yourself before God. Now ponder a significant question you have about your life's direction (if you took up a question in Exercise 1 and need more time with it, continue your discernment; or choose a different issue). Pose your question to God. It may be helpful to imagine asking Jesus. Remain in silence, open to what comes. Don't try to think of an answer. Just allow images, impressions, words, scripture phrases, feelings, and intuitions to surface. As these arise, note them in your journal. Offer thanks to God for any new insight into your question.

EXERCISE 4

Read Psalm 131. This short psalm expresses the wisdom of resting in quiet trust, with childlike confidence in God's loving presence and sure guidance. It begins with the individual and ends by commending this same stance to the whole community of faith.

Once again take up an unresolved issue in your life for which you seek clarity (it may or may not be the same one you identified in Exercise 1 or 3). This time, go for a walk where you can see grass, trees, and sky. Open yourself to divine perspective by observing what comes to you from the natural world. Carry your question with you and be alert to any clues you receive from God's creation that speak to your condition.

When you return, note fresh perspectives or insights in your journal. If you feel so moved, sing a song of joy and praise to God.

EXERCISE 5

Read John 13:34-35. Jesus says we will be recognized as his disciples by our love for one another. He asks us to love one another the same way he has loved us. We can only grow into such love over time, with clear intention, much practice, and perseverance.

Our chapter ended with the image of communal discernment as a dance. We were invited to think about discernment not simply as discreet decisions but as a whole *lifestyle* of faithful listening and response. Learning to love one another as Christ loves us is certainly a new lifestyle.

Stand and find space where your body can move freely. Close your eyes and think back over the past few days about your interactions with family members, coworkers, church members, friends, or strangers. Take one situation where you would like to have responded with more love. Slowly relive this encounter, inviting the Spirit to guide your thoughts, words, and gestures to reflect Christ's love. Allow your mouth to speak and your body to move as the Spirit governs. Then choose another interaction you would like to relive in the love of Christ, and let your body move again to the rhythm of grace. Do this several times, and begin to feel the dance of the Spirit repatterning your heart and hands. To end, let your body express thanks to God through gesture or movement.

Week 9
Elements of Perpetual Challenge

Then he said to them all, "If any want to become my followers,
let them deny themselves and take up their cross daily and follow me.
For those who want to save their life will lose it,
and those who lose their life for my sake will save it."

—Luke 9:23-24

As we journey in the way of discernment, we sometimes find ourselves greatly challenged by the direction we begin to discern. Two stories illustrating this reality come to mind. With intense clarity they show where discernment can lead.

The first story involves North Church, a multiracial congregation located in the predominantly African-American section of a midwestern city. Despite chronic financial uncertainties, the church for many years fostered special ministries among the poor. During citywide conflict over school integration in the 1960s and 1970s, members maintained a steady witness to racial harmony and justice in the name of Christ. They also established a food pantry that grew into one of the city's largest independent social service agencies.

In the late 1980s, the congregation sought to discern afresh where God was leading. The church had long included in its membership persons living with chronic mental illness. It now became clear that God was calling the congregation to expand its ministry with this largely neglected part of the human family. This meant doing more than just saying, "Everyone is welcome here." The pastor and members visited group homes for the mentally ill. They learned the intricacies of the public mental health care system. They related to families of the mentally ill, who had their own deep needs. As time passed, worship changed to allow for

Discernment is about hearing God's call in the midst of where one serves, whatever the context.

—Margaret Benefiel

the particular requirements of these newer members of the congregation and also for their abundant gifts. Persons living with mental illness started to serve on the boards of elders and deacons.

"God called us into a whole new world," one longtime member told me as he spoke of the change that had taken place. "That world lay right on our doorstep, but we had never seen it. Once we entered, we met suffering and pain, but above all, Jesus' love in ways we never expected."

The member paused for a moment after saying this, apparently working something through in his mind. Then he completed his thought: "I'll have to be honest. It was a challenge!" He looked directly at me and smiled, but said nothing more. The warmth of his smile embraced the goodness of all that had happened and also the immense challenge of the adjustments, time, and learning that had been required.

The second story is brief and harsh. I was at home with my parents the summer between graduation from college and entering seminary. One evening my mother called to me from the living room: "It just came over the television. Your friend Jack has been badly beaten." This was in the mid-1960s. Jack was taking part in the voter registration campaign conducted by the Southern Christian Leadership Conference. The news item was over by the time I got into the room.

Jack had prayerfully discerned his call to register voters as part of a nonviolent Christian effort for major change among disenfranchised black voters. Later that night, we learned that when he was beaten, Jack had not fought back. He simply tried to collapse onto the ground. His family expressed no hatred toward those who beat him when they were interviewed the next day. Nor did Jack in words he spoke a week later while recovering. He had followed where God's gift of discernment guided him. He was at peace about that. It was clear, though, that discernment had drawn him to a place of great threat and physical pain.

I have long pondered both of these stories. I am convinced they offer something even more vital than the appropriate insight, "Faithful discernment can lead us into difficult and risky situations." That body of believers seeking God's will for North Church and my friend Jack were in touch with two perpetually challenging elements in discernment: the prophetic cry and the cross. When we rightly understand and faithfully respond to these elements, they will stretch us greatly. No matter how

We are urging what is a seeming impossibility—a training to the use of non-violent means of opposing injustice, servitude. . . . It is again the Folly of the Cross. But how else is the Word of God to be kept alive in the world[?]
—Dorothy Day

many times we encounter them, they never lose their demand. "When I hear the prophetic cry inviting me to respond to some searing need in the human community, my stomach churns," a much older friend told me years ago. "That cry forever disturbs my peace. And as for the cross, it never loses its pain, not if you really carry it."

The prophetic cry. The cross. The farther we journey in the way of discernment, the more we realize that we must live with both, for they are integrally related. To keep growing as discerning persons, it is essential to reflect on each and how to live faithfully with both.

Responding to the Prophetic Cry

We meet the prophetic cry many places in the scriptures. Even a brief survey reveals its sweeping nature and insistent force. Amos, speaking a sharp word of the Lord (5:23-24), issues a summons to justice in the land of Israel:

> Take away from me the noise of your songs;
>   I will not listen to the melody of your harps.
> But let justice roll down like waters,
>   and righteousness like an ever-flowing stream.

Isaiah (58:6-7) extends this call with images that embrace the needs of the oppressed, the hungry, the homeless, and the naked:

> Is not this the fast that I choose:
>   to loose the bonds of injustice,
>   to undo the thongs of the yoke,
>   to let the oppressed go free,
>   and to break every yoke?
> Is it not to share your bread with the hungry,
>   and bring the homeless poor into your house;
> when you see the naked, to cover them,
>   and not to hide yourself from your own kin?

In softer tones, Micah issues the same cry and binds it to our daily walk with God (6:8):

> [God] has told you, O mortal, what is good;
>   and what does the LORD require of you

In the Bible, faith is not something you possess but rather something you practice. You have to put it into action or it really doesn't mean anything. Faith changes things. It's the energy of transformation, both for individuals and for a society.

—Jim Wallis

but to do justice, and to love kindness,
and to walk humbly with your God?

The prophetic cry comes as a relentless summons to bear God's wholeness and peace into the world's brokenness and strife. To respond to this cry is to walk humbly with God and build up the reign of Christ. It is to stand for justice, meet the needs of the poor, and advocate for the forgotten and the victims of discrimination.

The prophetic cry sounds across the ages and calls forth both our prayers and our deeds. Methodist minister Ernest Fremont Tittle, one of the great prophetic voices of the twentieth century, accented the fullness of this call in his commentary on the Lord's Prayer:

> To pray *thy kingdom come* is to pray for a new mind, a new heart, new interests and aims and purposes. It is to pray for an end to bitter poverty in the midst of potential plenty, an end to human exploitation, racial discrimination, and war. . . . It is to pray for a world so organized that nations will not impoverish and degrade themselves in insane attempts to destroy one another.[1]

In Tittle's view, the ultimate voice for the prophetic cry was Jesus, who showed that our prayers for God's new order must become incarnate in our deeds. Jesus challenged those who would follow him to give themselves wholeheartedly to the hurting, the poor, the rejected (Matt. 25:31-46; Luke 18:18-23). With festive meals and pointed parables, he expanded his listeners' understanding of who was welcome in God's family, urging them to adopt the radical, open love of God's kingdom (Mark 2:13-17; Luke 10:25-37).

How can we respond faithfully to the prophetic cry? We may find this a particularly vexing question. The call to bear God's new order into the world sounds from many different quarters. At times we feel overwhelmed, wondering, *How do we even know where to begin?* In response, I have heard two pieces of counsel. Each has helped me. They have helped others too, and I share them with gratitude.

The man who said of the prophetic cry, "That cry forever disturbs my peace" was living wholeheartedly the first item of counsel: "Hear the cry from scripture, from Jesus, from voices of daring and pain in your own age. As you listen, let that cry disturb you." He could have

According to the Bible, it is central to the very nature of God to demand justice for the poor and oppressed.
— Ronald J. Sider

You can't just watch from the sidelines. You have to come onstage. You are part of the community now. You have to venture, to risk.
—Robert McAfee Brown

ignored the cry and gone blissfully about his business. Instead, he chose to listen and take on the inevitable discomfort. Attentive discomfort is never easy, but it marks the beginning of a faithful response.

However, this first counsel does not resolve the larger issue. With so many voices calling and so many needs confronting us, how do we know where to respond? Here everything we have been learning in *The Way of Discernment* comes into play. Whether we are acting as individuals or as a group, we need to pause and get deeply in touch with our particular gifts in Christ. We need to consider potential fruits, to weigh prayerfully the genuine movements of desolation, consolation, and peace in our hearts. My own temptation is to do the opposite. I want to rush ahead, responding to this specific need, then to another and yet another. In the end, I exhaust myself and still feel guilty for what I have not done. The second counsel for responding faithfully to the prophetic cry offers a gentler, richer way: "Pause. Prayerfully take time to discern the particular call God is giving you."

The people of North Church followed both pieces of counsel for responding faithfully to the prophetic cry. They let the cry disturb them. They took time, prayerfully discerned their specific call, and responded with a focused effort that fit their ample gifts. My friend Jack did the same when he gave his summer and nearly his life to the cause of civil rights. If we respond faithfully to the prophetic cry, we may, in the words of theologian Maria Harris, be drawn into work "as ordinary as caring for our children . . . as unusual as teaching fish-farming to India's rural poor . . . as play-filled as a game of basketball and as serious as burying our dead."[2] In our haste-driven age, we may find ourselves summoned to proclaim blessings that will come only as we slow our pace and draw from the spiritual wellsprings of the living God. Answers to the prophetic cry abound. To find our particular answer, we need to let that cry unsettle us, then stop in our tracks and prayerfully discern what God sets before us.

Avoid being dominated by human timetables; it is God's time, not our time, that is our concern.
—Suzanne Farnham et al.

Bearing the Cross

Sometimes what God sets before us is unmistakably the cross. Spiritual guide Thomas Green notes that those who most willingly follow the Lord will be guided to respond to concrete needs around them, and such faithfulness will inevitably lead to times of bearing their own cross.[3] Indeed, those who discern the leadership of the risen Christ come to view the cross not just as the sign of a long-ago event, but as an immediate burden they must take up and carry as they follow Jesus into the world. This surely was so for my friend Jack. The bruises on his flesh and the blood from his open wounds were marks of the cross.

The cross may take subtler forms as well. An engineer discerns God's call to speak out against dangerous practices in his company. He says what he needs to at a meeting of his department. The next week he notices that his supervisor and several others ignore him. After a month he wonders, *Do I even have a future here?* Three young women in a prayer group initiate biweekly dialogues with young women of another faith. They do this because they discern dialogue as a way to follow Jesus' call to love their neighbors and build up God's new order in the world. The women of both faiths find much in common. They grow close. Together they explore how to raise children without prejudice. Back in their congregation, the three women endure pointed questions and sharp comments. "Why are you associating with them?" "Remember, you are a Christian! Don't lose your roots."

"If any want to become my followers," Jesus said, "let them deny themselves and take up their cross and follow me" (Mark 8:34). I find these words particularly blunt. Jesus leaves no escape clause. The cross is for everyone who seeks to follow him. We may need time to discern whether a particular cross is ours to carry, just as we need time to discern how to answer the prophetic call. Or we may not have the luxury of time. Either way, as we faithfully seek to follow Jesus' leadership for our lives, a key question becomes: What perspective can aid us when we know we must carry the cross?

Few contemporary Christians have written so poignantly about bearing the cross as Dietrich Bonhoeffer, the German pastor executed by the Nazis in 1945. In his classic work *The Cost of Discipleship*, Bonhoeffer articulates a key perspective for all whose discernment brings them to the cross. "To endure the cross," he writes, "is not a tragedy; it is the suffering which is the fruit of an exclusive allegiance to Jesus Christ."[4] Jesus is the reason for carrying the cross. Allegiance to him is what brings on the cross in the first place, and allegiance to him makes carrying it worth

Will our actions, if we follow through with our decisions, reflect Christ or not?
—Jeannette Bakke

How about giving up safety for Lent?
—Rick Ufford-Chase

the cost. Those who bear the cross may suffer rejection by others, but Bonhoeffer notes this is "rejection for the sake of Christ."[5] They may endure pain, but they do so knowing they serve the One whose healing love overcomes all pain, injustice, and even terror. My friend from North Church put all this so gently, describing what the people of that congregation encountered as they followed Jesus' lead along a difficult path: "We met suffering and pain, but above all, Jesus' love in ways we never expected."

My friend's words, like Bonhoeffer's finely honed perspective, remind me: *allegiance to Jesus Christ, with his overwhelming, world-healing love, is the reason for carrying the cross.* When I strain under the relatively minor burdens I must bear, a wider vision stretches me. "Look," I hear within my spirit. "This is what it is all about. Stay with it. You are following the Risen One who calls you and is even now making all things new!" This reminder in turn lifts my eyes. I begin to see others: my friend Jack; the engineer who suffered because he spoke a needed truth in his workplace; the three women who ventured into dialogue with women of another faith. And I see congregations willing to sacrifice comfort to follow in the way Jesus leads them. I soon envision a whole band of such folk, a "great . . . cloud of witnesses" (Heb. 12:1) surrounding and encouraging me. Not one of them says it is easy, but not one puts down the cross. They appear in touch with assurances far greater than the challenge of the cross, assurances we will explore in the final week of this study. For the moment, though, I simply need to ponder their faithfulness. They prize their bond with the risen Lord above all else, so they follow even when he leads them into the harshest realms.

Let me preach [to] you without preaching, not by words but by my example, by the catching force, the sympathetic influence of what I do, the evident fullness of the love my heart bears to you. Amen.

— Mother Teresa

DAILY EXERCISES

Read Week 9, "Elements of Perpetual Challenge." Keep your journal nearby to note impressions, feelings, insights, and struggles that surface as you read the article and work through the daily exercises. Stay wide open to the Spirit as you move deeper into the prophetic and corporate dimensions of discernment.

Exercise 1

Read Isaiah 58:6-7. Here the prophet reinterprets to Israel the fast that pleases God: not refraining from certain foods but refraining from presumptions of superiority, desire to control others, and habits of inattention to human need.

Meditate on the part of you that says yes to these words, that draws your spirit with a sense of deep truth. Recall times when you felt the sting of injustice, felt oppressed or marginalized in some way, hungered for something you couldn't get, physically or emotionally. Express your feelings nonverbally in movements, gestures, even groans.

Now reflect on the part of you that says no to this passage, that feels uncomfortable or irritated with it. Recall times you encountered others in need and failed to respond fully. Identify feelings (fear, uncertainty, helplessness) that urge you to resist the prophetic cry. Find a way to express these feelings also in movements/gestures/sounds.

Observe the similarities and differences in your feelings, gestures, and groans. Let them carry you into prayer. Wrestle with the Voice behind the prophetic word. As insights come, note them in your journal.

Exercise 2

Read Micah 6:8. Read it again slowly. These words speak clearly and simply to three central dimensions of God's will—the divine intention and yearning for us all. Engage this passage creatively in *one* of the following ways:

(a) Gather scissors, glue, and several old magazines or newspapers. Cut out images or headlines that speak to you of (1) doing justice, (2) loving kindness, and (3) walking humbly with God. Create a small collage for each theme on separate journal pages or larger pieces of paper.

(b) Reflect: How have you, someone you know, or your church expressed each of these central dimensions of God's will? In your journal, sketch an image or symbol for each of the three categories (artistic ability is not necessary; the idea is to sketch just general or symbolic expressions). You might add words or people's names to the images.

Offer your creation to God in prayer, asking to be shown one concrete way to grow personally in each essential expression of the divine will. Note insights that come, and pray for strength to act on what you hear.

EXERCISE 3

Read Matthew 16:21-26. Jesus is clear that his cross-bearing and suffering for our sake will involve those who follow him in suffering for his sake. As disciples we are privileged to share in his sufferings, thus in his ongoing redemptive work through the church in this world.

Reflect on your life and people or churches you have known. Where have you seen or experienced "bearing the cross" for Jesus' sake? What faithful actions have resulted in disapproval, derision, or hostility from people in or outside the church? Write in your journal what you recall.

Now breathe deeply and relax into quiet. Under the loving gaze of God, ask: Is there a situation in my life where I sense a call to respond more faithfully to the way of Christ—a response that could cost me something I am reluctant to give up (time, comfort, reputation, approval, job)? As thoughts, impressions, and feelings surface, note them in your journal. Pray for courage and wisdom to act on any clear direction you may receive.

EXERCISE 4

Read Philippians 3:7-11. Paul considers his suffering for Christ's sake a small thing compared to "the surpassing value of knowing Christ Jesus." The motive behind Paul's desire to become "like him in his death" is to "know Christ and the power of his resurrection." The apostle keeps a big, joyful picture before his eyes in every trial.

Reflect on this text in one of the following ways:

(a) How have you been called to enter death in order to know the power of resurrection? List the "deaths" that have been required of you,

even if they seem small. What have you had to let go of that was truly precious to you, or what hurts have you endured? Then consider what new life you have seen emerge, internally or externally, from dying to part of yourself. Write about the larger joyful picture you can authentically hold in your trials.

(b) Ponder what you most fear about "the cost of discipleship" and what you most affirm about the value of following Jesus. Then take a walk with your journal in hand. Carry your struggles and affirmations with you in prayer as you walk. Open yourself to perspectives that come from what you observe in the world around you. Jot down your insights.

EXERCISE 5

Read Hebrews 13:12-16. Three forms of sacrifice are named in these verses: (1) the physical sacrifice of suffering, like Jesus, for the sake of faithful witness to God's truth; (2) the sacrifice of praise to God, which involves confessing Christ's name; (3) the sacrifice of doing good and sharing what we have with those in need.

Ponder how these elements of sacrifice mix together in your own life. If you drew them as circles, how large would each be, and would they intersect? Does one dimension stand out, or seem absent? Identify any patterns you see and note or draw them in your journal.

When you have "carried the cross," how has the experience deepened your praise or given meaning to your outreaching generosity? Let your reflections take you into prayer.

Week 10
The All-Encompassing Assurance

And remember, I am with you always, to the end of the age.
—Matthew 28:20

The seasoned pastor grew excited as she neared the climax of her third sermon to this new congregation. Faces turned upward. Eyes looked expectant. Even George, who claimed the last pew on the right and had slept peacefully through her two previous efforts, looked alert. *The Holy Spirit is working!* she sensed. Responding to a somewhat undefined inner prompting, she laid aside the rest of her carefully prepared manuscript. Now she had no idea where she was going with the sermon.

She paused and looked over the congregation. She paused a bit longer, still clueless regarding where to go next. The congregation began to realize she was casting about, but waited patiently.

The sermon had focused on the last four verses of the Gospel of Matthew and had portrayed Jesus' appearance to the eleven disciples on a mountain. Several times she spoke Jesus' words urging the eleven to go forth and make disciples of all nations. Through a dramatic monologue, she had probed the inner thoughts of several in this astonished group of followers.

Now she was stuck. She thought a bit more, then gingerly drew on her own feelings of the moment. "Those poor disciples had no idea where they were going. Well," she said, hesitating a little, "all they had were Jesus' words at the end of the Gospel: '*And remember, I am with you always, to the end of the age.*'"

Just as she said this, her eyes fell on the face of an older man who had stopped by her office earlier that week. His wife had died six months ago. He was grieving, didn't know which way to turn with his life, faced important decisions about what to do with his ample talents and about possibly moving to be closer to his children, but he was unsure about any of this. He desperately needed to talk. She had listened, and the two had prayed. She looked away from him and out over the congregation.

"And remember, I am with you always, to the end of the age!" she repeated.

The preacher's eyes then rested for just a moment on a single mom in her late teens. She also had stopped by the office this past week, and the two had prayed. The teenager had made poor choices in her relationships and now struggled to make better ones, hold a job, and care for the child she loved dearly. She was bright and gifted, but parenting, making right choices, and sticking to them were so hard. The pastor gently looked elsewhere, then spoke with strength:

"Remember, I am with you always, to the end of the age."

Now another parishioner came to mind. She could not see the man at the moment but had glimpsed him with his wife and two children entering the sanctuary before worship. She had met him only briefly, but even then found him remarkably at peace. "He's got a rotten, tough job," the church's Chief Source of Unsolicited Information had told her. "We can't figure out why he left the good position he had, but that's not our business. Maybe you'd like to ask him." Somewhere out there sat this peace-filled man with the rotten, tough job. The pastor scanned the congregation and called out once more, "Jesus said to the disciples, and he says to us all, *'Remember, I am with you always, to the end of the age.'*"

The congregation heard the depths from which she spoke. She stayed silent for just a moment longer, and then continued slowly: "That's enough for now. Let the people of God say, 'Amen.'" And the entire congregation, even George in the last pew on the right, said, "Amen!"

*   *   *

> *We are able to rest, in the words of an old hymn, "on the promises," we are willing to lean "on the everlasting arms."*
> —Kathleen Norris

The undergirding reality for every step along the way of discernment is the divine assurance: "I am with you. I will be with you always." As we noted last week, the challenges we face in our journey of faithfulness can be immense. Yet through each challenge, Jesus still speaks his word, "I am with you always." This divine assurance addresses us in our uncertainty. It enfolds us in our wondering. It reminds us that if we live discerning lives, we will find ourselves continuously upheld by the One who gifts us with discernment and sustains us in the ways we are called to follow. The divine assurance encompasses all the paths we have traversed till now and all that lie ahead of us. It meets us over and over in the most foundational elements of our life together as Christians: the biblical word, the waters of baptism, and the bread and cup shared by our Lord. In our final chapter of *The Way of Discernment*, we will explore this assurance, especially as it comes to us through the perpetually present gifts of Word and Sacrament.

Assurance in Scripture

In scripture, the divine "I will be with you" takes on more forms than our minds can trace. Yet if we pause to dig even briefly into the biblical word, we see how deeply rooted this divine assurance is and how utterly without limit. The prophet Isaiah, speaking the word of the Lord, cries out:

> Do not fear, for I have redeemed you;
>   I have called you by name, you are mine.
> When you pass through the waters, *I will be with you*;
>   and through the rivers, they shall not overwhelm you.
>   —Isaiah 43:1-2, emphasis added

The God of love knows each of us intimately. Even in the hardest places God claims us, sustains us, and brings us through.

Jeremiah speaks to our anxiety over finding the pathway to God: "When you search for me, you will find me; if you seek me with all your heart, I will let you find me, says the Lord" (Jer. 29:13-14). Centuries later, Jesus offers that same assurance even more plainly: "Ask, and it will be given you; search, and you will find; knock, and the door will be opened for you" (Matt. 7:7).

The divine assurance in scripture extends not only to our times of turbulence, self-doubt, and anxiety over finding the right way. Ultimately it enfolds even our death, as the apostle Paul proclaims:

While all the powers of Good aid and attend us boldly we'll face the future, be it what may.
—Dietrich Bonhoeffer

For I am convinced that neither death, nor life, nor angels, nor rulers, not things present, nor things to come, nor powers, nor height, nor depth, nor anything else in all creation, will be able to separate us from the love of God in Christ Jesus our Lord. (Romans 8:38-39)

Paul hides nothing from his readers. Death is real for them, as it is for him. So too are life's seasons of spiritual turmoil, pain, and dark wondering. But more real, and infinitely more abiding, is the assurance that "in all these things we are more than conquerors through him who loved us" (Rom. 8:37).

The divine assurance found in scripture can speak with simple power and great specificity. Years ago I sat beside a middle-aged man facing an operation that carried substantial risk and, if he survived, the guarantee of a long, painful recovery. He could have declined the procedure, but he had prayerfully discerned that for him and his family this was the course to follow. He looked at me just before being wheeled off to surgery. "The Lord is my shepherd," he said. "I shall not want." He smiled and gave my hand a firm squeeze. That scriptural assurance accompanied him as he disappeared behind the operating room doors. It glowed through him in the months of recovery that followed. Had the surgery gone differently, I am convinced that he still would have found the divine assurance completely fulfilled.

Then there was what the pastor of our opening story heard from the peace-filled man with the "rotten, tough job." She did not ask him about it. He soon volunteered over coffee that for a decade he had coached several sports at a community college. The pay was good, and the students were "mostly terrific." Then he learned of the need for somebody to coach and counsel disturbed teenagers in the roughest section of the city. He felt drawn to this new situation, and his wife supported him as he entered a time of prayerful discernment. "A lot of people said I was crazy if I left what I had, but I was excited about using my gifts in that environment. I also kept hearing Jesus' promise that if we leave what is familiar and comfortable for his sake, he will fill our lives a hundred-fold with new parents and brothers and sisters and children. I went ahead, took the step, and what Jesus said is *exactly* what happened."[1] He laughed. "Some still think I'm crazy, but our whole family is richer. We are learning so much. I wouldn't trade this job for anything."

> *When I really think it through, it has all been a single road to God. Do not grieve that I must now skip the last part of it. Soon I shall be closer to you than before. In the meantime I'll prepare a glorious reception for you all.*
> —Christoph Probst

The divine assurance we find in scripture speaks to our particular needs as we aim to live discerning lives. Whenever I learn of others who have heard the assurance, their experience invites me to listen more closely to the biblical word myself. Their faithfulness reminds me that I need to ask, "What passages of scripture most lift and assure me right now as I walk in the way of discernment?"

Assurance Through Water, Bread, and Cup

I once watched a group of Sunday school second graders perform a brief play titled *How Was You Baptized?* Their teacher had adapted it from an ancient and regrettably now out-of-print curriculum. The skit began with a bunch of cowboys and cowgirls seated around a campfire. "How was you baptized?" one of them asked. "Sprinkled as a baby," said three of them. "Sprinkled as a baby?!" answered three others. "That's not right! We was dunked at twelve!" "Dunked? That's not right!" said the first three. At this, all leapt to their feet and drew their six-shooters. "WAIT! WAIT!" called out a tall girl with a commanding voice. "Don't you see? You're *all* baptized. At the very least," she was talking like a firm parent, "that means God loves every one of you, and it means you all belong together." "Oh, that's wonderful!" said the others, putting down their six-shooters. They locked arms like pals and giggled all the way back to their pew.

In all the years since, I have never found the sequel to that play. I muse that with tidied-up language it could have been *How Do You Take the Bread and Cup?* Like its predecessor, this dramatic gem would acknowledge that we followers of Jesus have varied the patterns and language by which we celebrate these priceless gifts. And those presenting the play would end with that powerful, assuring note sounded by the adult voice in their midst: "*At the very least*, these gifts mean that God loves every one of you, and all of you belong together."

The children in that original play have entered middle age now. I count it one of life's great joys that I still know what three of them are up to. In varied ways, they are doing good, exciting things with their lives. I hope and pray that this is true as well for the others who shared that skit. I would like to believe they too have encountered ever richer

> *Scripture is central to discerning call. . . . As the living Word of God, Scripture continues to communicate to us.*
>
> —Suzanne Farnham et al.

assurance from the waters of baptism and the hallowed gifts of bread and cup.

I hope the richness of assurance for these now middle-aged children has included the knowledge that at baptism they were drawn into new life in Christ and that there are no limits to the growth they can find in this life (Rom. 6:3-4; Col. 2:12). They carry with them now the mark and guarantee of their true identity: they are beloved of God and drawn daily into growing union with Christ. In Christ they become cherished community together. They are truly one (Eph. 4:4-6).

I also hope that the richness these persons find in the bread and cup is heightened by awareness that Christ steadily feeds them in spirit through these physical signs, and that even now the nourishment they receive springs up to eternal life as Christ abides in them and they in Christ (John 6:53-58). Moreover, I trust that a simple assurance underlies all the blessings these baptized, nurtured ones now experience. Dorothy Day, a tireless Christian reformer through much of the twentieth century, expressed that assurance in these words: "There is this question, why did Christ institute this Sacrament of his Body and Blood? And the answer is simple. It was because he loved us and wished to be with us."[2]

Christ loves us and wants to be with us.

"And remember, I am with you always, to the end of the age."

It is Wednesday as I write these words. Four more days and I will join others as they enter an aging, much-loved sanctuary for worship. I will carry with me my praise and thanksgiving, my questions and uncertainties, and my yearning to follow Jesus in ways that share God's love. Others entering the sanctuary will do the same. I expect that somewhere slightly gray heads that years ago asked, "How was you baptized?" will also enter sanctuaries. The signs of assurance will be right there for us all, wherever we join in worship. They will greet us this Sunday even if no one is baptized, even if we don't hear the words "This is my body. This is my blood." We will see the signs as we pass a baptismal pool or font, view a chalice and plate upon table or altar, or simply carry images in our minds: The waters of baptism. The bread and the cup. As we enter the embrace of God's love, these gifts never leave us. In all the joys and agonies of discerning our path forward in life, they speak the assurance

You are, in truth, the true nourishment of the soul, and he who worthily receives You will be partaker and heir of eternal glory.
—Thomas à Kempis

that proclaims: "I love you. I have claimed and marked you. I will feed and sustain you. I will guide and direct your steps. I am with you always, as you all journey together. Come! Keep walking in the way I lead you."

Postscript—A Return to Desire

For ten weeks we have considered *The Way of Discernment.* At the outset, we noted that before we even hear the word *discernment,* its reality beckons us. It calls to us through our deep desire to walk in ways that are whole, right, and fitting for who we truly are—the persons God made us to be. That desire burns hot when we struggle with difficult choices, deal with life's changes, or simply seek to live faithfully Jesus' life-giving way in the world. We have spent time exploring how discernment comes as gift in response to our seeking—both personally and in the life we share together. We have considered many ways to open ourselves to receive the gift. We have acknowledged that faithful acceptance of this gift will draw us into much joy but also into great challenge. And now we hear the all-encompassing assurance of the living Christ who is with us always and will draw us to himself through all things.

I meditate on this all-encompassing assurance. As I consider the limitless love from which it flows, I find I am cast back to the very beginning, except with a whole new level of awareness. I encounter afresh in me the desire—the enticing, persistent desire—to discern still more fully how I can follow in the way of the One who so steadily calls and so faithfully loves.

The habitual attitude of discernment . . . is a way of gradually coming to live out of our desire for God in all of life.
—Rose Mary Dougherty

DAILY EXERCISES

Read Week 10, "The All-Encompassing Assurance." Use your journal to capture insights, hopes, prayers, and sketches as you read the article and respond to each daily exercise. Note any ways these responses connect you with earlier weeks, and with your *Companions in Christ* group. Seek the assuring, beckoning company of the risen Lord through this week as you prepare for the final meeting of your group.

EXERCISE 1

Read Matthew 28:16-20. Commissioning his band of apostles to make faithful disciples throughout the world, the risen Lord promises to support their labors with his constant spiritual presence, guidance, and strength. Reread the last sentence several times, hearing it addressed to you personally. Allow the word *always* to resonate until the assurance of this promise feels rooted in your soul.

Where have you most sensed Jesus' active presence with you through these weeks in *The Way of Discernment?* Note responses in your journal.

Now think of what has most challenged you over these weeks, or where you feel stirred to respond to Christ's call more faithfully. Allow Jesus' promise of continual presence to speak to you as you hold this challenge or call in prayer.

EXERCISE 2

Begin by quieting yourself in God's love. Then prayerfully ask yourself what passages of scripture speak to you of the divine promise "I will be with you."

Write phrases or passages as best you can recall them, verses you turn to for comfort, courage, assurance, or peace. Look them up in your Bible if you know where they are, or use a concordance. You might return to the chapter for some options.

Select one verse or passage that especially speaks to your heart. Shape it into a breath prayer you can easily say and remember. Repeat this prayer gently, receiving it as a word of God to your soul. Then write your verse or prayer on a small card to carry with you or place visibly as a daily reminder of the divine assurance.

EXERCISE 3

Read Romans 8:31-39. This beloved passage expresses Paul's most profound assurance of God's eternally present love for us in Christ.

Where in your life do you most need to hold close the promise that nothing can separate you from the love of Christ? Respond in your journal. Then examine any specific anxieties you have around discerning God's will in your life, such as fears about where faithful obedience to Christ might lead you. Name these in writing.

Immerse yourself in the promise of Romans 8, especially verses 35, 38-39. Let the sense of assurance wash over all your fears until you feel at peace. Find a symbol of this divine assurance—for example, a feather, cross, rock, or piece of fabric—to help you face the challenges before you. Put this symbol in a place where you can see and touch it daily.

EXERCISE 4

Read John 6:56-63. Jesus interprets to his disciples the inner meaning of this difficult teaching: his "flesh and blood" represent "spirit and life." In baptism we are joined to Christ's life spiritually and united with his body, the church. In Holy Communion we are repeatedly nourished in this "new creation" life, personally and corporately.

Ponder what baptism and the Lord's Supper mean to you. How do they connect you with Jesus' "spirit and life"? Write your thoughts. Then sketch an image of your relationship with Christ and his community.

If you have time, ponder a few circumstances in your life when you received "true food" according to your need. Jot down words describing the circumstance and note beside them the spiritual food you received (courage, mercy, peace, knowledge, hope, joy). You may feel moved to express your gratitude through song or simple movement.

EXERCISE 5

Read Ezekiel 36:26-28. The prophet speaks the divine promise to give a new heart and spirit to the people of Israel—a heart after God's own heart and a spirit willing to follow God's ways.

Prayerfully ask: Where, in the past ten weeks, has God been resculpting my heart from stone to flesh? How has my spirit been made new? What patterns can I detect in my life that may reveal the new heart and spirit God is giving me? Pray for insight and journal about your reflections. It may help to draw an image symbolizing the new spirit or new patterns you see emerging.

Finally, ponder where your journey through these weeks has taken you in terms of desire for God. How has your spiritual yearning been strengthened or stretched? Offer your desire and hope to God in prayer, and give thanks!

Notes

WEEK 1

1. Thomas H. Green, *Weeds Among the Wheat—Discernment: Where Prayer and Action Meet* (Notre Dame, IN: Ave Maria Press, 1984), 22.

WEEK 2

1. Paul Anderson, "The Present Leadership of the Resurrected Lord," *Evangelical Friend* 23:7/8 (1990): 2–3, 19; later reprinted in pamphlet form (Newberg, OR: Barclay Press) and posted online at http://www.georgefox.edu/discernment/present_leadership.pdf.

2. Dr. Gordon Smith presented the concept of relating to Jesus in real time at a conference on Discerning the Leadership of Christ, sponsored by George Fox University, January 16–18, 2005.

3. Thomas N. Hart, *The Art of Christian Listening* (New York: Paulist Press, 1980), 84.

4. Ignatius of Loyola, *The Spiritual Exercises of St. Ignatius: Based on Studies in the Language of the Autograph*, trans. Louis J. Puhl (Chicago: Loyola University Press, 1951), 71.

5. Hart, *The Art of Christian Listening*, 85.

6. Green, *Weeds Among the Wheat*, 49.

WEEK 3

1. Dag Hammarskjöld, *Markings*, trans. Leif Sjöberg and W. H. Auden (New York: Alfred A. Knopf, 1964), 93.

2. Tracy Kidder, *Mountains Beyond Mountains: The Quest of Dr. Paul Farmer, A Man Who Would Cure the World* (New York: Random House, 2004), 211.

3. William A. Barry and William J. Connolly, *The Practice of Spiritual Direction* (New York: Seabury Press, 1983), 115.

4. Patricia Loring, *Listening Spirituality*, vol. 1, *Personal Spiritual Practices Among Friends* (Washington, DC: Openings Press, 1997), 125.

Week 4

1. "Living someone else's life" is a frequent theme in the writings of counselor James Hollis. Readers may be particularly interested in James Hollis, *Creating a Life: Finding Your Individual Path* (Toronto: Inner City Books, 2001).

2. Rose Mary Dougherty, *Group Spiritual Direction: Community for Discernment* (New York: Paulist Press, 1995), 30.

Week 5

1. James Finley, *Merton's Palace of Nowhere*, rev. ed. (Notre Dame, IN: Ave Maria Press, 2003), 114.

2 . *Peace Pilgrim: Her Life and Work in Her Own Words* (Santa Fe, NM: Ocean Tree Books, 1991), 11. Both this question and the third arise from the reflections of Nancy Reeves in her essay "How Do I Know It's God?" in Nancy Reeves, *I'd Say Yes, God, If I Knew What You Wanted: Spiritual Discernment* (Kelowna, BC: Northstone Publishing: 2001), 74–76.

3. Hart, *The Art of Christian Listening*, 83. Bracketed words are mine.

4. Gerald G. May, *Will and Spirit: A Contemplative Psychology* (San Francisco: Harper & Row, 1982), 6.

5. Green, *Weeds Among the Wheat*, 174.

Week 6

1. Holly W. Whitcomb, *Seven Spiritual Gifts of Waiting* (Minneapolis: Augsburg Books, 2005), 102.

2. For a full treatment of these biblical texts and the theme of waiting, see Stephen V. Doughty, "Adrift," in *Weavings: A Journal of the Christian Spiritual Life* 14, no. 2 (March–April 2001), 16–22.

3. Reeves, *I'd Say Yes, God, If I Knew What You Wanted*, 210.

4. Ignatius of Loyola, *The Spiritual Exercises of St. Ignatius*, trans. Louis J. Puhl (Chicago: Loyola University, 1960), paragraph 318, 142–43.

Week 7

1. Charles M. Olsen, *Transforming Church Boards into Communities of Spiritual Leaders* (Bethesda, MD: Alban Institute, 1995), 89.

2. Suzanne G. Farnham, Stephanie A. Hull, and R. Taylor McLean, *Grounded in God: Listening Hearts Discernment for Group Deliberations,* rev. ed. (Harrisburg, PA: Morehouse Publishing, 1999), 33.

3. Valerie K. Isenhower and Judith A. Todd, *Discernment into Transformation: A Guide to Corporate Spiritual Discernment* (Albuquerque, NM: Water in the Desert Ministries, 2006), 4.

4. Gordon Smith, lecture at "Discerning the Leadership of Christ" conference sponsored by George Fox University at Colorado Springs, January 16–18, 2005.

5. Readers may wish to explore Wendy M. Wright's essays in *Companions in Christ: A Small-Group Experience in Spiritual Formation* (Nashville: Upper Room Books, 2001), part 5, "Exploring Spiritual Guidance," Weeks 2 and 3.

6. A beautiful, practical delineation of this form of group guidance is available in Rose Mary Dougherty, *Group Spiritual Direction: Community for Discernment* (New York: Paulist Press, 1995).

7. For a full treatment of the Clearness Committee, see Parker J. Palmer's article "The Clearness Committee: A Way of Discernment" in *Communion, Community, Commonweal: Readings for Spiritual Leadership,* ed. John S. Mogabgab (Nashville, TN: Upper Room Books, 1995), 131–36.

WEEK 8

1. *Morality in American Agriculture: A Few Practical Reflections for Laypeople and Their Ministers* (printed and distributed through the Presbytery of Northern New York, 1974; promoted through the Interfaith Center of Corporate Responsibility, New York, NY). The authors were the farm folk who participated in the exploration.

2. Rachel Naomi Remen, *Kitchen Table Wisdom: Stories That Heal* (New York: Riverhead Books, 1996), 293.

3. Readers wishing to further explore communal discernment will find practical help in any of the following resources: Farnham, Hull, and McLean, *Grounded in God: Listening Hearts Discernment for Group Deliberations* (Harrisburg, PA: Morehouse Publishing, 1999); Isenhower and Todd, *Discernment into Transformation: A Guide to Corporate Spiritual Discernment* (Albuquerque, NM: Water in the Desert Ministries, 2006—available from Water in the Desert Ministries, P. O. Box 65818, Albuquerque, NM 87193); Danny E. Morris and Charles M. Olsen, *Discerning God's Will Together: A Spiritual Practice for the Church* (Nashville: Upper Room Books, 1997); chapter 5, "Seeing with Spiritual Eyes: The Practice of Prayerful Discernment" in Charles Olsen, *Transforming Church Boards* (Bethesda, MD: Alban Publications, 1995); Charles M. Olsen and Ellen Morseth, *Selecting Church Leaders: A Practice in Spiritual Discernment* (Nashville: Upper Room Books, 2002).

4. In the Wesleyan (Methodist) heritage, these four key arenas are called the Quadrilateral—scripture, tradition, reason, and experience.

WEEK 9

1. Ernest Fremont Tittle, *The Gospel According to Luke: Exposition and Application* (New York: Harper & Brothers, 1951), 121.

2. Maria Harris, *Proclaim Jubilee! A Spirituality for the Twenty-first Century* (Louisville, KY: Westminster/John Knox Press, 1996), 109–110.

3. Green, *Weeds Among the Wheat*, 175.

4. Dietrich Bonhoeffer, *The Cost of Discipleship*, rev. and unabridged (New York: Macmillan, 1959), 78.

5. Ibid.

WEEK 10

1. Mark 10:29-30.

2. Dorothy Day, *In My Own Words,* ed. and comp. Phyllis Zagano (Liguori, MO: Liguori Publications, 2003), 16. The quotation originally appeared in an editorial by Dorothy Day in *The Catholic Worker*, September 1934.

Sources and Authors of Margin Quotes

WEEK 1

Soetken van den Houte, in *Golden Apples in Silver Bowls: The Rediscovery of Redeeming Love*, trans. Elizabeth Bender and Leonard Gross, ed. Leonard Gross (Lancaster, PA: Lancaster Mennonite Historical Society, 1999), 153.

Jeannette A. Bakke, *Holy Invitations: Exploring Spiritual Direction* (Grand Rapids, MI: Baker Books, 2000), 218.

Rose Mary Dougherty, *Group Spiritual Direction: Community for Discernment* (New York: Paulist Press, 1995), 24.

Saint Augustine, *Confessions*, trans. Henry Chadwick (New York: Oxford University Press, 1991), 3.

Dougherty, *Group Spiritual Direction,* 25.

Malcolm Muggeridge, *The Infernal Grove*, vol. 2 of *Chronicles of Wasted Time* (New York: William Morrow & Co., 1974), 272.

WEEK 2

Gerald G. May, *Will and Spirit: A Contemplative Psychology* (San Francisco: Harper & Row, 1982), 290.

Danny E. Morris and Charles M. Olsen, *Discerning God's Will Together: A Spiritual Practice for the Church* (Nashville: Upper Room Books, 1997), 16.

Nancy Reeves, *I'd Say Yes, God, If I Knew What You Wanted* (Kelowna, BC: Northstone Publishing, 2001), 19.

Ibid. (capturing an image from Catherine of Siena), 35.

Dougherty, *Group Spiritual Direction*, 25.

Ibid., quoting Saint Ignatius of Loyola.

Danny E. Morris, *Yearning to Know God's Will* (Grand Rapids, MI: Zondervan, 1991), 29–30.

Bakke, *Holy Invitations*, 218.

WEEK 3

Bakke, *Holy Invitations*, 222.

Ibid.

Suzanne G. Farnham et al., *Listening Hearts: Discerning Call in Community,* rev. ed. (Harrisburg, PA: Morehouse Publishing, 1991), 24.

Mother Teresa of Calcutta, quoted in *Pocket Book of Prayers*, comp. M. Basil Pennington (New York: Image Books, 1986), 132.

Farnham et al., *Listening Hearts*, 12.

Reeves, *I'd Say Yes, God, . . .*, 18.

WEEK 4

Dietrich Bonhoeffer, "Who Am I?" in *Prisoner for God: Letters and Papers from Prison,* ed. Eberhard Bethge and trans. Reginald H. Fuller (New York: Macmillan, 1958), 165.

James Finley, *Merton's Palace of Nowhere,* rev. ed. (Notre Dame, IN: Ave Maria Press, 2003), 96.

Ibid., 46.

Farnham et al., *Listening Hearts*, 36.

Bakke, *Holy Invitations*, 225.

WEEK 5

Bakke, *Holy Invitations*, 212.

Dougherty, *Group Spiritual Direction*, 25.

Thomas H. Green, *Weeds Among the Wheat—Discernment: Where Prayer and Action Meet* (Notre Dame, IN: Ave Maria Press, 1978), 178.

Bakke, *Holy Invitations*, 223.

Henri J. M. Nouwen, *With Open Hands* (Notre Dame, IN: Ave Maria Press, 1972), 154.

Dag Hammarskjöld, *Markings*, trans. Leif Sjöberg and W. H. Auden (New York: Alfred A. Knopf, 1964), 90.

Bakke, *Holy Invitations*, 229.

WEEK 6

George Croly, "Spirit of God, Descend upon My Heart," in *The Presbyterian Hymnal: Hymns, Psalms, and Spiritual Songs* (Louisville, KY: Westminster/John Knox Press, 1990), no. 326.

Holly W. Whitcomb, *Seven Spiritual Gifts of Waiting* (Minneapolis: Augsburg Books, 2005), 88.

Margaret Benefiel, *Soul at Work: Spiritual Leadership in Organizations* (New York: Church Publishing, 2005), 56.

Morris and Olsen, *Discerning God's Will Together*, 90.

Ignatius of Loyola, *The Spiritual Exercises of St. Ignatius*, trans. Louis J. Puhl (Chicago: Loyola University Press, 1960), 143.

Bakke, *Holy Invitations*, 222.

Dougherty, *Group Spiritual Direction*, 32.

Katharina von Schlegel, "Be Still, My Soul," trans. Jane Laurie Borthwick, in *The Hymnbook* (Richmond, VA: Presbyterian Church in the U.S., Presbyterian Church in the U.S.A., United Presbyterian Church in North America, Reformed Church in America, 1955), no. 374.

WEEK 7

Morris and Olsen, *Discerning God's Will Together*, 13.

Farnham et al., *Listening Hearts*, 58.

Morris and Olsen, *Discerning God's Will Together*, 14.

Reeves, *I'd Say Yes, God . . .*, 89.

Victoria Grace Curtiss, "Discernment and Decision-Making" in *The Final Report of the Theological Task Force on Peace, Unity, and Purity of the Church* (Louisville, KY: Presbyterian Church [U.S.A.], 2006). This article is available as a PDF at http://www.pcusa.org.

Bakke, *Holy Invitations*, 223.

Paul Anderson, "The Present Leadership of the Resurrected Lord," *Evangelical Friend* 23:7/8 (1990): 2–3, 19; later reprinted in pamphlet form (Newberg, OR: Barclay Press) and posted online at http://www.georgefox.edu/discernment/present_leadership.pdf.

Dougherty, *Group Spiritual Direction*, 37, commenting on small-group application of Julian of Norwich's description of praying for a friend.

Ibid., 24.

WEEK 8

Morris and Olsen, *Discerning God's Will Together*, 14.

Farnham et al., *Listening Hearts*, 62.

Morris and Olsen, *Discerning God's Will Together*, 15.

Curtiss, "Discernment and Decision-Making," 1.

Farnham et al., *Listening Hearts*, 61.

Morris and Olsen, *Discerning God's Will Together*, 14.

Benefiel, *Soul at Work*, 56.

Ibid., 57.

John E. Anderson, quoted in Curtiss, "Discernment and Decision-Making."

WEEK 9

Benefiel, *Soul at Work*, 53.

Dorothy Day, *In My Own Words*, ed. and comp. Phyllis Zagano (Liguori, MO: Liguori Publications, 2003), 37.

Jim Wallis, *Faith Works: Lessons from the Life of an Activist Preacher* (New York: Random House, 2000), xxviii.

Ronald J. Sider, *Rich Christians in an Age of Hunger: Moving from Affluence to Generosity*, 4th ed. (Dallas: Word Publishing, 1997).

Robert McAfee Brown, *Spirituality and Liberation: Overcoming the Great Fallacy* (Philadelphia: Westminster Press, 1988), 153.

Farnham et al., *Listening Hearts*, 48.

Bakke, *Holy Invitations*, 224.

Rick Ufford-Chase, Moderator of the Presbyterian Church (USA), in sermon delivered at Western Theological Seminary, March 11, 2006.

Mother Teresa of Calcutta, quoted in *Pocket Book of Prayers*, comp. M. Basil Pennington (New York: Image Books, 1986), 132.

WEEK 10

Kathleen Norris, *The Cloister Walk* (New York: Riverhead Books, 1996), 382.

Dietrich Bonhoeffer, "New Year (1945)," in *Prisoner for God: Letters and Papers from Prison*, ed. Eberhard Bethge and trans. Reginald H. Fuller (New York: Macmillan, 1958), 187.

Christoph Probst, in Alan Paton, *Instrument of Thy Peace* (New York: Seabury Press, 1968), 117.

Farnham et al., *Listening Hearts*, 32.

Thomas à Kempis, *The Imitation of Christ*, trans. Richard Whitford and ed. Harold C. Gardiner (Garden City, NY: Image Books, 1955), 210.

Dougherty, *Group Spiritual Direction*, 33.

Resources

The following list contains information about the Companions in Christ series, books quoted from in *The Way of Discernment,* and resources that expand on the material in this book. As you read and share with your group, you may find some material that particularly challenges or helps you. This list may be useful if you wish to pursue individual reading on your own or if your small group wishes to follow up with additional resources. Unless otherwise indicated, these books can be ordered at www.upperroom.org/bookstore/ or by calling 1-800-972-0433.

THE COMPANIONS IN CHRIST SERIES
Companions in Christ: A Small-Group Experience in Spiritual Formation (Participant's Book, #0914) by Gerrit Scott Dawson, Adele J. Gonzalez, E. Glenn Hinson, Rueben P. Job, Marjorie J. Thompson, and Wendy M. Wright

Companions in Christ: A Small-Group Experience in Spiritual Formation (Leader's Guide, #0915) by Stephen D. Bryant, Janice T. Grana, and Marjorie J. Thompson

The Way of Grace (Participant's Book, #9878) by John Indermark; (Leader's Guide, #9879) by Marjorie J. Thompson and Melissa Tidwell

The Way of Blessedness (Participant's Book, #0992) by Marjorie J. Thompson and Stephen D. Bryant; (Leader's Guide, #0994) by Stephen D. Bryant

The Way of Forgiveness (Participant's Book, #0980) by Marjorie J. Thompson; (Leader's Guide, #0981) by Stephen D. Bryant and Marjorie J. Thompson

The Way of Transforming Discipleship (Participant's Book, #9842) by Trevor Hudson and Stephen D. Bryant; (Leader's Guide, #9841) by Stephen D. Bryant

The Way of Prayer (Participant's Book, #9906) by Jane E. Vennard with Stephen D. Bryant; (Leader's Guide, #9907) by Marjorie J. Thompson

Exploring the Way: An Introduction to the Spiritual Journey (Participant's Book, #9806) by Marjorie J. Thompson; (Leader's Guide, #9807) by Marjorie J. Thompson and Stephen D. Bryant

The Way of the Child by Wynn McGregor
Leader's Guide and Sessions   #9824
Family Booklet   #9839

Resource Booklet   #9825
Music CD   #9845
Training DVD   #9846
Church Pack   #9847

The Way of the Child focuses on the spiritual formation of children ages 6–11. Part of the Companions in Christ series, it helps children learn and experience spiritual practices that will lead them into a deeper awareness of God's presence in their lives. The Leader's Guide includes five chapters on the spiritual nature of children and theory of faith formation as well as thirty-nine sessions to use with groups of children. There are enough sessions to use from September through May in Sunday school or weekday or weeknight settings. This resource is also designed for short-term use such as during Advent, Lent, or other special times of the year.

Journal: A Companion for Your Quiet Time #938
Introduction by Anne Broyles
Generous space for writing, faint lines to guide your journaling, and a layflat binding. Many pages contain inspirational thoughts to encourage your time of reflection.

OTHER RESOURCES OF INTEREST

The Upper Room Dictionary of Christian Spiritual Formation
by Keith Beasley-Topliffe
Nearly five hundred articles cover the people, methods, and concepts associated with spiritual formation, with a primary emphasis on prayer and other spiritual disciplines. #0993

Alive Now
With a mix of prayers, award-winning poetry, stories of personal experience, and contributions from well-known authors, *Alive Now* offers readers a fresh perspective on living faithfully. Available as an individual subscription or group order.

Weavings: A Journal of the Christian Spiritual Life
Through thoughtful exploration of enduring spiritual life themes, *Weavings* offers trustworthy guidance on the journey to greater love for God and neighbor.

Clapper, Gregory S. *Living Your Heart's Desire: God's Call and Your Vocation*. Nashville: Upper Room Books, 2005.

Dougherty, Rose Mary. *Group Spiritual Direction: Community for Discernment*. New York: Paulist Press, 1995.

Farnham, Suzanne G., Stephanie A. Hull, and R. Taylor McLean. *Grounded in God: Listening Hearts Discernment for Group Deliberations*. Rev. ed. Harrisburg, PA: Morehouse Publishing, 1999.

Isenhower, Valerie K. and Judith A. Todd. *Living into the Answers: A Workbook for Personal Spiritual Discernment*. Nashville: Upper Room Books, 2008.

Isenhower, Valerie K. and Judith A. Todd. *Listen for God's Leading: A Workbook for Corporate Spiritual Discernment*. Nashville: Upper Room Books, 2009. [Until 2009 this book is available under the title *Discernment into Transformation: A Guide to Corporate Spiri-*

tual Discernment—from Water in the Desert Ministries, P.O. Box 65818, Albuquerque, NM 87193.]

Jones, W. Paul. *The Art of Spiritual Direction: Giving and Receiving Spiritual Guidance.* Nashville: Upper Room Books, 2002.

Mogabgab, John S., ed. *Communion, Community, Commonweal: Readings for Spiritual Leadership.* Nashville: Upper Room Books, 1995. No longer in print but available online through used bookstores.

Morris, Danny E. and Charles M. Olsen. *Discerning God's Will Together: A Spiritual Practice for the Church.* Nashville: Upper Room Books, 1997.

Olsen, Charles M. "Seeing with Spiritual Eyes: The Practice of Prayerful Discernment." In *Transforming Church Boards.* Bethesda, MD: Alban Institute, 1995.

Olsen, Charles M. and Ellen Morseth. *Selecting Church Leaders: A Practice in Spiritual Discernment.* Nashville: Upper Room Books, 2002.

Wuellner, Flora Slosson. *Enter by the Gate: Jesus' 7 Guidelines When Making Hard Choices.* Nashville: Upper Room Books, 2004.

About the Authors

Stephen V. Doughty is the author of numerous essays and four books, including *To Walk in Integrity* and *Discovering Community* from Upper Room Books. A graduate of the two-year program in spiritual guidance offered by the Shalem Institute for Spiritual Formation, Steve pastored congregations in the St. Lawrence River Valley, the Black Hills, and Appalachia and served as a regional denominational executive for ten years. He frequently leads retreats and conferences.

An ordained minister of the Presbyterian Church (USA), Doughty holds two degrees from Yale University Divinity School and a B.A. from Williams College. He and his wife, Jean, live in Otsego, Michigan, where they are just minutes from enjoying two of their favorite activities: canoeing and hiking.

Marjorie J. Thompson, creator of the daily exercises, brings over twenty-five years of experience with retreat work, teaching, and writing in the area of Christian spiritual formation to her work as director of Pathways in Congregational Spirituality with Upper Room Ministries. She is the author of *Soul Feast: An Invitation to the Christian Spiritual Life* and *Family, The Forming Center*. An ordained minister in the Presbyterian Church (USA), Marjorie has served in pastoral ministry and as adjunct instructor in several seminary settings.